| Biblical Refigurations

Samuel and the Shaping of Tradition

BIBLICAL REFIGURATIONS

General Editors: James Crossley and Francesca Stavrakopoulou

This innovative series offers new perspectives on the textual, cultural, and interpretative contexts of particular biblical characters, inviting readers to take a fresh look at the methodologies of Biblical Studies. Individual volumes employ different critical methods including social-scientific criticism, critical theory, historical criticism, reception history, postcolonialism, and gender studies, while subjects include both prominent and lesser-known figures from the Hebrew Bible and the New Testament.

Published Titles Include:

Jeremy Schipper *Disability and Isaiah's Suffering Servant*
Keith Bodner *Jeroboam's Royal Drama*

SAMUEL AND THE SHAPING OF TRADITION

MARK LEUCHTER

UNIVERSITY PRESS

Great Clarendon Street, Oxford OX2 6DP
United Kingdom
Oxford University Press is a department of the University of Oxford.
It furthers the University's objective of excellence in research, scholarship,
and education by publishing worldwide. Oxford is a registered trade mark of
Oxford University Press in the UK and in certain other countries

© Mark Leuchter 2013

The moral rights of the author have been asserted

First Edition published in 2013
Reprinted 2014

All rights reserved. No part of this publication may be reproduced, stored in
a retrieval system, or transmitted, in any form or by any means, without the
prior permission in writing of Oxford University Press, or as expressly permitted
by law, by licence or under terms agreed with the appropriate reprographics
rights organization. Enquiries concerning reproduction outside the scope of the
above should be sent to the Rights Department, Oxford University Press, at the
address above

You must not circulate this work in any other form
and you must impose this same condition on any acquirer

Published in the United States of America by Oxford University Press
198 Madison Avenue, New York, NY 10016, United States of America

British Library Cataloguing in Publication Data
Data available

Library of Congress Cataloging in Publication Data
Data available

ISBN 978-0-19-965933-3

Links to third party websites are provided by Oxford in good faith and
for information only. Oxford disclaims any responsibility for the materials
contained in any third party website referenced in this work.

Acknowledgments

This book began over a bean burrito. Jeremy Schipper and I were having lunch and I was lamenting having to spend the afternoon working on a book project that did not at all excite me. Over the course of the burrito I was eating, he convinced me to table the boring project and write something that would keep me interested. Later that afternoon, I sat down and started writing what would become one of the chapters of this book. I am thankful for Professor Schipper's sage wisdom then and since. I also owe a serious debt of gratitude to Jeremy Hutton. Working with Professor Hutton on the SBL Levites and Priests sessions (and co-editing a collection of essays on that topic) helped solidify many of the avenues of inquiry I followed while writing this book. His critical acumen and encyclopedic knowledge were invaluable resources as this project evolved.

I must thank Francesca Stavrakopoulou for inviting me to submit this work to the Biblical Refigurations series. Her insight helped me devise a trajectory and scope for the book, and she made it a pleasure to move the project from the proposal stage to the writing of the manuscript. This process was also helped by the heroic generosity of Keith Bodner, who has also contributed a volume to this series and whose suggestions and encouragement made my own task much easier. The folks at Oxford University Press were a delight to work with as well—I thank Tom Perridge and Elizabeth Robottom for their patience and flexibility, especially toward the tail end of this enterprise.

Several ideas in this book resulted from my participation in a number of scholarly seminars and groups. In particular, the Columbia Hebrew Bible Seminar at Columbia University and the Old Testament Research Colloquium at Princeton Theological Seminary provided stimulating environments to throw some things at the wall and see what would stick. I must thank my colleagues at the University of Sydney for hosting me in the summers of 2009 and 2010 as a visiting professor, during which time I presented papers that formed the basis for much of what is now found in chapters 3 and 4 of this book. I am also grateful to John Kloppenborg at the Centre for the Study of Religion at University of Toronto, who arranged for me to have access to the university's library resources during the summer of 2011, when much of this book was written.

Along the way, the knowledge of many trusted colleagues proved a great help. Thanks to Alex Jassen, Diana Edelman, Anselm Hagedorn, Simi Chavel, Seth Sanders, Bill Schniedewind, Gary Rendsburg, Jacob Wright, Chip Dobbs-Allsopp, Yael Avrahami, Ben Sommer, Baruch Halpern, and Saul Olyan for their input. I am fortunate for the encouragement of my colleagues in the department of Religion at Temple University, who made it so enjoyable to come into the office every day and work on this book. And I am especially fortunate for my students, both graduate and undergraduate, who let me talk about the contents of the book as it was coming together and who asked questions that moved me to continue to dig deeper.

Finally, I want to thank my wife Sari. I started writing this book while staying with her in July–August 2011, and despite my nerding it up that summer and in the months that followed, she still said yes when I asked her to marry me. Sari, thanks for being patient, funny, kind, and loving, for tolerating my obsession with Rush, and for observing that the Chronicler would make the worst superhero ever. The bird is the word, but this book is for you.

Contents

Introduction	1
1. Viewing Samuel through a Deuteronomistic Lens	13
2. Samuel as a Levite	22
3. Samuel as a Prophet	41
4. Samuel as a Judge	63
Conclusion: Samuel in Biblical and Extra-Biblical Perspective	83
Notes	99
Bibliography	139
General Index	153
Scripture Index	155

| *Introduction*

> Wheels within wheels in a spiral array,
> A pattern so grand and complex...
>
> —Rush, "Natural Science"

The study of the book of Samuel remains a dependable bastion of scholarly disagreement.[1] Linguists debate whether or not its contents can be used to chart the development of biblical Hebrew, text critics argue over the priority of the different manuscript versions of the book, historians bicker over how distant its authors stood from the events they depicted (or if those events ever took place), literary critics plumb the depths of the narrative for thematic and dialogical weight, and perhaps more than any other brand of scholar, redaction critics forage the text's compositional strata for signs of sources and how they were brought together. For any scholar aspiring to write on the book of Samuel at the outset of the 21st century, the flurry of scholarship is overwhelming. Fortunately, there is a distinction to be drawn between the book of Samuel and the literary figure after whom it is named. For while the former has been at the epicenter of biblical scholarship for over a century, the latter has not received the attention he deserves.

Part of the reason for this is that within the book of Samuel, most of the narrative's attention is devoted to the figures of Saul and David, and the lion's share of that attention is granted to David's rise to power and the drama surrounding his family.[2] In a work that contains fifty-five chapters (1 Sam 1–31; 2 Sam 1–24), only a small amount of those are exclusively concerned with the character of Samuel in his own right. And even these chapters, it has often been argued, have been shaped with an eye to what unfurls later with both Saul and David.[3]

This is explainable if one recognizes that the sources in the book of Samuel have their primary roots in the Israelite royal court or were shaped to reflect upon Israel's monarchic legacy.[4] The authors or redactors of the book recruit the figure of Samuel to serve a royal agenda of some sort, regardless of whether that agenda is for or against kingship. However, as Frank Moore Cross stated decades ago, prophecy (as an institution distinct from the royally sponsored priesthood) and monarchy rose together; if Samuel obtained high rank in the pantheon of Israel's prophets—as the biblical record repeatedly attests—it is because he was woven into the narrative of that monarchic state's infancy.[5]

A brief look at Samuel in the service of two opposing royal houses

An example of how Samuel was appropriated by the shapers of royal agenda appears in the pro-Saul narrative spanning 1 Samuel 9:1–10:16. The narrative was conceived to cast Saul in the most positive light, and the authors behind it felt that this could be best accomplished via Samuel's sacral agency.[6] The *bamah* banquet in 1 Samuel 9:22–4 is especially revealing in this regard:

And Samuel took Saul and his servant, and brought them into the chamber, and made them sit in the best place among those in attendance, who were about thirty persons. And Samuel said to the cook: 'bring the portion I gave you, of which I said to you: set it aside.' And the cook took up the thigh, and that which was upon it, and set it before Saul. And [Samuel] said: 'Behold that which has been reserved! Set it before yourself and eat; because it has been kept for you until the appointed time, for I said: I have invited the people.' So Saul ate with Samuel that day.

Jonathan Jacobs has recently drawn attention to this episode as a turning point in the narrative, where it becomes clear to Saul that his meeting with Samuel is a matter of divine provenance for which Samuel and his company were prepared.[7] But the literary role of this banquet highlights the sociological ramifications of Saul being invited into Samuel's personal abode, granted pride of place at the table, and given Samuel's meal portion at the feast. This is not mere hospitality, but the ceding of sacral authority to the guest of honor. In other contexts, a ritual meal cements relationships and covenantal precepts shared between parties. In some cases, it is a priestly character who mediates between divine and human parties, and in others, the ritual meal is conducted by the divine figure himself.[8] With Samuel kowtowing to Saul in this episode, we encounter a decisive passing of the torch.[9] Saul quite literally becomes master of the house—Samuel's and, implicitly, those of the clan kinship groups who had hitherto deferred to the latter's authority.

The pro-Saul authors of the tale have deftly exploited a staple of sacral praxis to make a case for the changing of the guard. By the end of the tale, the change has indeed begun to take place: it is Saul, not Samuel, who now encounters the divine, is overcome by the spirit of God and moved to join a nearby band of cultic prophets (1 Sam 10:10–12).[10] Such a qualification provides a suitable antecedent and justification for later events such as 1 Samuel 13:9, 14:35 (and, possibly, 15:9), and 1 Samuel 22, where Saul appears to take measures to helm the cult of the realm.[11]

The account of Samuel's encounter with David (1 Sam 16:1–13) also relies upon Samuel's role as the chief representative of the sacral caste, but carries a very different tone.[12] While the Saul narrative points ahead to Saul's own interest as royal patron and chief over the cult, the very opposite obtains in the account of David's selection by Samuel:

And Samuel did that which YHWH spoke, and came to Bethlehem. And the elders of the city came to meet him trembling (*wayyeheredu*), and said: 'do you come peaceably?' And he said: 'Peaceably I come to sacrifice to YHWH; sanctify yourselves and come with me to the sacrifice.' And he sanctified Jesse and his sons, and called them to the sacrifice. (1 Sam 16:3–5)

In contrast to Saul's proactive nature as he traverses his future realm in 1 Samuel 9:1–10:16, it is Samuel who journeys south to Judah.[13] As he approaches, the elders of Bethlehem recognize his authority and tremble (*wayyeheredu*). The root *hrd* here does not connote fear but religious awe, similar to the reaction of the nation at Sinai (Exod 19:16) and, later, the pious in relation to the divine word (Isa 66:2; Ezra 9:4)... such piety is present in Bethlehem at the sight of Samuel. Samuel then instructs the elders to sanctify themselves; though the specifics of this term are not spelled out, the elders maintained a degree of religious responsibility within the paradigm of Samuel's authority and presence.

This brief exchange reveals what the narrator must have intended to be the "proper" sacral dynamic in the old hinterland culture, with sacral leadership maintaining the order and infrastructure of local kinship groups and their religious initiatives and duties.[14] Implicitly, David is presented as coming from a social universe where figures such as Samuel are revered, and his ongoing interaction with Samuel in the ensuing chapters emphasizes the importance of priestly/prophetic cooperation in ruling the populations of the central highlands.[15]

In both cases, Samuel is deployed strategically to justify the authors' respective arguments. It is undeniable that we encounter here competing agendas and the subordination of Samuel to those agendas by later writers. Nevertheless, Zechariah Kallai has made the case that in the creation of historiography, genuine historical circumstances set the parameters for how those circumstances are taken up by subsequent writers.[16] Biblical texts, especially historiographies, are reactions to events. Even if those reactions are burdened by agenda or bias, they may still help the scholar gain a sense of how those events were recalled and utilized for ideological discourse in Israelite antiquity. This applies to individuals as well—these examples both serve as reactions to traditions about Samuel that point to a dominant role he held in Israelite imagination regarding the early days of kingship.

The biblical sources in literary profile

With regard to the literary recollection and utilization of Samuel, four sources in the Hebrew Bible stand out: the book of Samuel (1 Sam in particular), a few mentions in the book of Chronicles (1–2 Chr), and brief references in Psalm 99 (v. 6) and Jeremiah (Jer 15:1).[17] The book of Samuel receives the greatest attention from scholars and for good reason, for it provides the most extensive and detailed information, but within this literary whole are components that envision different worlds from different times. It is clear that the book of Samuel as it stands is a testament to centuries of composition, transmission, and adjustment.[18] Changes in social and political circumstances invariably shaded the narratives and the perception of Samuel himself. It is therefore impossible to imagine that even a well-established tradition or tale where Samuel plays a pivotal role would carry the same meaning from one generation of writers and audiences to the next as the book of Samuel grew over time and was read and, in the words of Ehud Ben Zvi, routinely re-read.[19]

The brief passages within the books of Chronicles, Psalms, and Jeremiah shed some light on the growth and interpretation of the Samuel tradition as it was re-read and re-written. For the Chronicler, Samuel is both prophet and Levite, and is instrumental in the planning of the Jerusalem temple—a view at odds with what the book of Samuel has to say. In Psalm 99 and Jeremiah, the emphasis differs, as Samuel is placed on par with no less than Moses as both priest (Ps 99:6) and prophet (Jer 15:1).[20] The authors behind the psalm and the Jeremiah passage have a very particular understanding of Samuel in mind that is not explicit in the book of Samuel.[21] This demands that the primary material in the book of Samuel be read cautiously; as we will see, clues may lurk therein as to how and why the Chronicler, the Psalmist, and Jeremiah identify these characteristics in their use of their sources.

Scholars such as Diana Edelman, Keith Bodner, and Roy Heller have noted that Samuel is by no means valorized by the biblical writers. In several cases, the writer highlights his personal shortcomings and chooses terms that reveal a complex and problematic character.[22] This has led some to the conclusion that the depiction of Samuel as a literary character carries a critique of prophecy as well.[23] However, a complex characterization of Samuel as an individual does not necessarily constitute an impugning of prophecy as an *institution*. Texts such as 1 Kings 13 argue the very opposite, namely, that the importance of prophecy as an institution transcends the foibles and errors of individual prophets. Even Moses, the greatest of Israel's prophetic figures, is cast in critical light from time to time, though it is ultimately his teachings that dominate as the highest standard of faith and obedience in the Pentateuch.

The promotion of prophecy alongside critical observations of prophets is part of a more general tendency regarding characterization within the Hebrew Bible. Whereas ancient non-Israelite documents often glorify the political leaders under whom they were composed, the biblical writers regularly highlight the humanity of figures from the past, revealing that the ideas these figures advanced were more important than the figures themselves. If Samuel periodically comes under fire for succumbing to his own humanity, it does not follow that this necessitates the writers' criticism of the ideas and social institutions he represents within the text.[24] The biblical writers make the distinction between these different dimensions of Samuel in their own work(s), identifying him as both a literary figure with his own all too human limitations while simultaneously utilizing him as a vehicle to advocate or criticize concepts that existed long before his day and which continued well beyond his demise.

Samuel as a liminal figure

Let us then consider briefly the complex literary picture of Samuel as he appears within the book carrying his name. He is a man both deeply connected to his family and yet positioned between them and the nation at large that follows his leadership.[25] He is the divinely chosen successor to a powerful and ancient priestly line, yet also the trustee of that priestly line's traditions. He stands at the intersection of an acephalous clan culture and the hierarchy of the nascent monarchy he inaugurates.[26] He is charged with preserving the conservative values of the past while also plotting out the future during a period of national transition. He is given the responsibility of inaugurating a king that YHWH has chosen and then, almost immediately, given the task of repealing that divine decision. In this, he claims to represent the voice of the divine just as he behaves in a manner that sometimes suggests his uncertainty in divine support. Even Samuel's name is an unresolved matter. In 1 Samuel 1:20, Samuel's Hebrew name, *šemu'el*, is explained as "I asked of him from YHWH,"[27] though etymologically, the name is better read as "his name is El"—denoting devotion to El as Israel's deity.[28] The narrative thus presents a character who is on the one hand derived from the realm of the divine while, on the other hand, a testament to human faith in that realm.

Joseph Blenkinsopp states that "the Samuel narratives are so overlaid with theological interpretation that it is now impossible to say anything certain about Samuel as a historical figure."[29] When one looks at the *Gestalt* of Samuel's literary depiction, he is liminal, standing in the space between diverse theological and political polarities, yet engaging them at various turns in the narrative. This reifies Blenkinsopp's view that the texts regarding Samuel have been highly over-written and are rendered opaque, with the character recruited to serve this-or-that ideology or purpose. Yet it is possible that the layers of interpretation he mentions not only create the impression of Samuel's liminality, but developed as a *result* of it. As per Kallai's historiographic observation above, we must consider the possibility that Samuel's literary liminality is the end result of pre-literary oral traditions about his leadership as deriving from liminal status.

Liminality is a major motif in Israelite self-conception. The Pentateuch presents Israel's national formation as taking place in the desert wilderness, the ultimate liminal space between the realm of the settled/sewn and the realm of cosmic chaos.[30] The nation comes into existence not simply through the liberation from Egypt, but through confronting its own demons and developing systems of social stability (law, the cultic fixtures of the Tabernacle, the priestly and lay leadership hierarchies) en route to the Promised Land. Through the language of symbolism and myth, this recalls in some way Israel's genuine origins, emerging on the one hand from lowland Canaanite culture of the late Bronze Age and, on the other, from the nomadic tribes of the Transjordan (e.g., the "sons of the east" in Gen 29:1).[31] Representatives of both social patrimonies became "Israel" once they claimed and cultivated the highland frontier of central Canaan between the tail end of the Late Bronze Age and the outset of the Iron Age (ca. 1250–1150 BCE). Indeed, Israel's place *between* these geographic and cultural contexts is the very thing that delineated their corporate identity as Israelites.[32]

If Israel defined itself by occupying a liminal position between lowland Canaanite and eastern nomadic groups, it is no wonder that liminality is emulated in later Israelite historiography. The sanctity of the concept is most forcefully evidenced by the Yahwistic poetry that shows a divine warrior long associated with the liminal space of the wilderness as the national patron deity (Exod 15; Judg 5:2–5; Ps 68; etc.),[33] but was grounded within the human realm as well. Gregory Mobley has drawn attention to this as an essential characteristic of Israelite heroism: the men who venture out to the steppe—and the battlefield—are channels for mythic archetypes concerning the divine warrior and that warrior's ability to confront and defeat cosmic challenges.[34]

Memory and the shaping of tradition

The same understanding undergirds the sacral authority of Moses, who embodies the sanctity of liminality in Israelite imagination.

Ronald Hendel has argued that the consistent "betwixt and between" characterization of Moses suggests that he was remembered early on as carrying these qualities and that this in turn informed the choices of the biblical writers who constructed his literary image.[35] Moses' characterization in the Pentateuch does not create his liminal status as much as attest to it as a major feature of the pre-biblical traditions surrounding him.

It may be that the biblical writers inherited similar memories regarding Samuel,[36] which accounts for the diverse ways in which he, too, is characterized both within and beyond the book of Samuel. The different biblical writers could seize upon Samuel as a vehicle for their own voices if he was already understood to be one of Israel's sacred liminal figures, whose qualities reaffirmed the forces that brought the nation into existence. We may go a step further and consider the possibility that of the three basic roles or traditions associated with Samuel—that of priest, prophet, and judge[37]—one tradition was most closely associated with this memory and formed the basis for the others. The priestly tradition recommends itself, as the early priesthood in Israel was characterized by a liminal quality, both socially and geographically.[38] The memory of Samuel's priestly traits, I will argue, permitted subsequent writers to identify Samuel with different typologies.[39]

But if the memory of Samuel as a priest proved to be influential in his literary characterization, we are still left with pressing questions. How is it that Samuel managed to eclipse the Elide priests at Shiloh, the sanctuary where the biblical writers inform us that he received his training? How could a mere adept such as Samuel emerge as dominant over a priestly family that held power even before he was born, and what were the mechanisms by which such priestly power could be challenged and eventually retooled or re-allocated? Moreover, what does this tell us about the relationship between the priests and the public they served, and the symbolic role that priests played in early Israel's theological self-conception? And what might this have to do with the later tradition preserved in the book of Chronicles that Samuel was a Levite?

When turning to Samuel's place as a prophet, why do we find dissonant presentations of his prophetic function and authority? Why is it significant that his inaugural prophetic experience takes place at Shiloh, and in what way does this contribute to the relationship between prophecy and kingship in the minds of the biblical writers? How is it that Samuel is characterized in such strong prophetic terms when so much of what legitimizes him throughout the book of Samuel stands at odds with the words of the "classical" prophets such as Amos, Hosea, Micah, and Isaiah? In what way do the biblical writers attempt to frame Samuel as a predecessor to these 8th-century figures?

When looking to Samuel's role as a "judge," does the picture of Samuel conform to the presentation of judges elsewhere as adjudicators and interpreters of the laws found in the Pentateuch? If not, how closely does Samuel match the profile of the warrior–savior figures from the book of Judges?[40] How is the social world in the book of Judges consistent with that of Samuel, and in what way is the record of his activity anticipated by the events recorded in the narratives of the deliverers who preceded him? Of course, many scholars have pointed out such correspondences, but since it is only with Samuel that the era of the judges is brought to a conclusion, one may turn the question around—in what way does Samuel's role as a judge affect the presentation of his deliverer predecessors, and to what end? Whose interests are served by this qualification? And what is the effect of having the era of the monarchy commence under the guidance of the individual who personally closed the preceding era?

The scope and purpose of the present study

The literary depth and complexity created by the shaping of earlier sources concerning Samuel is not something that obtains solely at the final-form level of the narrative(s). Rich dimensions of meaning are forged through the conscious awareness of how, and why, the redactors have retained and transformed their source material. Brian Peckham's 1995 essay "Writing and Editing" argues that scribes called deliberate attention to their redactional incursions.[41] The redactor of sources creates a coherent work that still retains multivalent voices, and indeed highlights the moments where older lines of thought in the sources finally come to fruition within a new literary context. The final text creates new textures by virtue of the vitality of ideas upon which the redactor builds, and provides new ways of perceiving those sources interwoven into the literary whole.

As such, the present study will enter into a discussion of the relationship between later redactional work and earlier narrative sources or cultural memories to address how the character of Samuel emerges as emblematic of the diverse traditions enumerated above. Chapter 1, "Viewing Samuel through a Deuteronomistic Lens," will consider the scholarly model of a Deuteronomistic History and the modality of thought identified as "Deuteronomistic." These are terms that most often relate to the idea of a late redactional group that inherited and transformed earlier traditions into a historiographic work with a specific understanding of the past informed by the language and themes in the book of Deuteronomy. Yet these terms are often overused and deployed without clear definitions as to whom the Deuteronomists were and what constituted their literature. Our exploration of the various claims on Samuel's memory must begin with a definition of Deuteronomism as a concept, for it is through the exponents of this concept that the ultimate or penultimate forms of the Samuel narratives have reached modern audiences.

Chapter 2, "Samuel as a Levite," broaches the issue of Samuel's rise to priestly prominence at Shiloh by offering a tentative reconstruction of the Levites as a sacral caste intimately connected to Israel's early priestly traditions. The chapter will look behind the redactional layer of the narrative material and consider its points of contact with anthropological, linguistic, theological, and historical traces of earlier experience. Attention will be focused on how the Levite caste formed an interface between the agrarian public and the dominant priestly clans, and how the Samuel narratives recall this process, to explain Samuel's own rise as the major priestly figure of his day. Arising from this are important suggestions as to why Samuel became so central a character in subsequent historiographic efforts.

Chapter 3, "Samuel as a Prophet," builds upon the discussion in the previous chapter by examining the distinction between priests with oracular/prophetic characteristics and the emergence of a distinct prophetic class. Samuel's rise to priestly prominence is built around a prophetic revelation he receives, so prophecy serves priesthood in this earlier material. However, different categories eventually emerged that represented divergent spheres of prophetic conduct and responsibility. The tradents behind the Samuel narratives draw from the memory of how the prophetic sphere changed in the shadow of monarchic institutions over time. Yet the traditions were also shaped to resonate with the growing body of prophetic literature from the 8th-century prophets, who advanced ideas potentially at odds with older traditions of prophecy preserved in Samuel–Kings.[42] The end result is a more comprehensive understanding of prophecy and its function during periods of social crisis.

Chapter 4, "Samuel as a Judge," continues to build on the discussion in the previous chapters, and posits that both Levites and prophets carried juridical authority as YHWH's sacral agents. However, after exploring traditions of jurisprudence and biblical law, the chapter notes the difference between "judging" as a vehicle for legislative justice and the type of "judges" in the book of Judges, a typology that most scholars have extended to Samuel as well. On the surface, Samuel would appear to fit into this mold and follow precedents set within the book of Judges, but a closer examination reveals difficulties in adopting this view. Rather, the chapter addresses a deeper issue involved in the characterization of Samuel as a judge, and one that preserves an inner-Israelite cultural struggle from many centuries before the book of Samuel took on its penultimate form(s).

The conclusion of this study considers the implications of the previous chapters and evaluates how the collective presentation of Samuel was read, interpreted, and applied by later writers both within and beyond the Hebrew Bible. The Persian period texts such as Ezra-Nehemiah and Chronicles demonstrate that the picture of Samuel set a precedent for how subsequent writers could draw from this earlier tradition and apply it to their own purposes. The trend persists with Hellenistic texts such as Ben Sira and the Qumran Samuel Apochryphon, both of which use Samuel to draw communal and ethnic boundaries, and the Roman period sources (Pseudo-Philo, Josephus) which operate somewhat differently. Finally, the early Christian and Rabbinic sources will be evaluated in terms of their application of the canonical Samuel narratives to the construction of new political and mythological canons of their own. In all cases, the formation of new traditions rebuild Samuel in the image that best suited the needs of the writers and their audiences.

In what follows, I do not attempt to take account of every narrative in which Samuel figures prominently. Dramatic episodes such as 1 Samuel 19:18–24 or 1 Samuel 28 demand detailed examinations, and other scholars have produced such studies worthy of the reader's attention.[43] Rather, this study will restrict itself to a few select texts and will examine them as ways in which Samuel's liminality is used for the sake of advancing or adjusting a tradition or typology. The translations of Hebrew Bible passages in this study are based upon the JPS translation of the traditional Hebrew version (the Masoretic Text or MT). However, I offer periodic adjustments to these translations when alternate versions such as the Greek Septuagint (LXX) provide better alternatives, or when the JPS translation overlooks important nuances in the original Hebrew. This study will also employ simplified Hebrew transliterations, though some more detailed grammatic discussion will sometimes be utilized for purposes of clarity. Finally, the divine name will be rendered "YHWH" rather than spelled phonetically, following the traditional Hebrew consonantal spelling.

1

Viewing Samuel through a Deuteronomistic Lens

The lens between wishes and fact...
—Rush, "Between Sun and Moon"

Throughout this study, I will use the term "Deuteronomistic" many times, which requires comment. My analysis of the Samuel material will rely heavily upon the scholarly construct of a "Deuteronomistic History." For biblical scholars, this term relates to the idea of a work woven from different sources that spans Deuteronomy–Kings and that tells the tale of Israel's existence from the inheritance of their ancestral land until their exile from it under Babylon.[1] I will be making certain claims about the scribal circles responsible for this literature that most scholars refer to as the "Deuteronomists." This tradition has been rightly characterized as elusive and thus demands some detail regarding its historical origins, the social-location of its proponents, and its ideological underpinnings.[2] In what follows, I will attempt to make a case for my working understanding and assumption of what the term "Deuteronomistic" means, who the Deuteronomists were, and how the literature associated with this group developed.

Defining what constitutes a Deuteronomistic History, its point of origin, its sources, and the social location of its authors remains one of the most hotly contested areas of Hebrew Bible scholarship today. Scholarly views have ranged from grouping Deuteronomy–Joshua apart from the ensuing canonical material,[3] grouping Samuel–Kings as the unit in conversation with Deuteronomy (with other texts secondarily attached as part of a subsequent enterprise),[4] or qualifying the entirety of Genesis–Kings as a Deuteronomistic document with a cohesive structure and theological interest.[5] Recent sessions at the annual meetings of the Society of Biblical Literature regularly see papers delivered that question the viability of a Deuteronomistic History altogether, seeing instead far greater diversity than unity from one book to another that precludes the possibility of the model's useful persistence.[6]

For many scholars, however, the model of a Deuteronomistic History provides a useful entrée into the study of Joshua–Kings (or, alternately, Deuteronomy–Kings). The major theories regarding the production of this historiography alternately see a single exilic redactor of early sources, multiple exilic and/or post-exilic redactors, or a "double-redaction" starting in the late pre-exilic period and persisting into the exilic period by the same redactional circle.[7] This last model has been especially influential in North American scholarship, where it is common to see a Deuteronomistic History emerging in connection to the reign of King Josiah (640–609 BCE) and expanded in subsequent periods.[8] Variations on all of these models have been proposed, including stages of historiographic composition dating from well before Josiah's reign, though these can at best be viewed as antecedents to a Deuteronomistic History (the Prophetic Record, a Hezekian historiography, an Ephraimite history, etc.), not as an early version of it.[9] A Deuteronomistic History, by definition, requires direct intertextual engagement of some sort with the book of Deuteronomy, the latter of which could not have surfaced in some form until the mid 7th century BCE at the very earliest, or (more likely) in the last quarter of that century.[10]

There is much to recommend this basic model of a historiographic work surfacing in the late 7th century BCE; a full consideration is beyond the scope of the present discussion, but a few significant observations can be made. The very distinct break in the regnal evaluation formulae of kings after Josiah immediately points to a work that initially ended with an account of Josiah's reign. The kings who follow are subject to different standards that presuppose the exile, and the shift from pre-exilic to exilic conditions account for this, while Josiah and those who precede him are not systematically subjected to these criteria.[11] Furthermore, it seems that the majority of the arguments regarding the evaluation of historical events were written from the perspective of someone still living in the Judahite homeland.[12] This is evident not only from geographic descriptions, but also from the fundamental rhetorical interests of the work. For example, the projection of unacceptable Judahite religious praxes onto the fallen northern population in 2 Kings 17:7–23 makes the most sense from the perspective of a Judahite resident. One can imagine that an exilic writer would be more apt to directly critique the religious practices of his fellow exiles,[13] and this is indeed what one encounters within exilic works such as Jeremiah 26–45 or the oracles of Ezekiel.

The view that a late pre-exilic context accounts for the emergence of Deuteronomistic thought and literature thus remains reasonable, but identifying the Deuteronomists as royal court scribes requires reconsideration. The assumption of the Deuteronomistic History as a royal historiography has forced some scholars to posit major ideological divisions which may not be necessary. Bernard M. Levinson has noted important differences between Deuteronomy's vision of monarchy (Deut 17:14–20) and the presentation of monarchs in the book of Kings.[14] Yet by assuming that Josiah's scribes stand behind a pre-exilic edition of the Deuteronomistic History, this discrepancy has been interpreted as a subsequent appropriation of Deuteronomy's contents (a "Deuteronomistic" attitude), empowering the king in a way that Deuteronomy did not intend...an "ideological clash," in Levinson's words.[15] In this, Levinson envisions a sharp break in scribal intent and social orientation, despite the very close linguistic and theological trove of concepts shared by the "Deuteronomic" and "Deuteronomistic" literature.

Marvin A. Sweeney moves in the other direction in attempting to address the issue. Sweeney accepts the double-redaction theory and places the Deuteronomistic History in the hands of scribes from Josiah's court, but these same scribes, he argues, penned Deuteronomy.[16] Here, of course, the law of the king in Deut 17:14–20 stands out as problematic for the same reasons that Levinson and others articulated. To deal with this problem, Sweeney interprets the rhetoric of Deuteronomy as actually empowering a king like Josiah despite appearing to circumscribe the royal sphere and the imperatives that the king could claim.[17] This, he argues, reconciles the apparent limitations with the legislation demanding cultic centralization (Deuteronomy 12), an act credited to Josiah in 2 Kings 23 and one that the entirety of the Deuteronomistic History seems to anticipate. Sweeney's discussion highlights the passages in Deuteronomy that do seem to legitimize a centralization that would support royal interest. Yet his discussion of Deuteronomy 17:14–20 relies on what is *not* said regarding the king's royal potential in order to make this case, and it remains difficult to sideline the carefully worded terms of circumscription along with the removal of the king from other traditional realms of royal conduct.[18]

The aforementioned difficulties are avoided, though, if one accepts the possibility that some form of the Deuteronomistic History and the book of Deuteronomy were composed in the late pre-exilic period among a scribal group that interacted with the royal court, but which was not directly accountable to it. Though many scholars have adopted the view that only royal scribes possessed the literary resources and sophistication to create a complex historiography such as that spanning Joshua–Kings, this represents too limited a view of scribalism in the late pre-exilic period.[19] As has long been observed, the book of Deuteronomy possesses a deep interest in the Levite priesthood (see chapter 2 of the present study for more on the Levites), and it is among such priests that literacy in antiquity was traditionally rooted.[20] The royal court or royally sponsored temple was not the only place where scribal facility could be found, and there are good grounds for seeing Levites retaining a scribal tradition of their own.[21]

There is evidence that following the destruction of the northern kingdom of Israel in 721 BCE, some northern Levites settled in Jerusalem and obtained scribal positions in the royal administration of the 7th century.[22] This group of Levites possessed the skills required to produce sophisticated literature, and their proximity to the administrative infrastructure of Jerusalem provided them with the sources and resources from which to work. Yet their northern lineage roots both safeguarded them from longstanding ideological allegiances to the Judahite throne and—having emerged from a culture that survived the failure of kingship in the north—allowed them to cultivate a more skeptical view of monarchic viability. This accounts for the social vision of Deuteronomy regarding the role of the king as well as the Levite sensitivities and qualified tolerance of kingship in the Deuteronomistic History.[23] If Deuteronomy was therefore not a writ licensed by Josiah's court, we must consider the sequence and purpose of both the composition of Deuteronomy and the Deuteronomistic History in relation to the events surrounding that king's reign, including a centralization effort that was most likely viewed by the rural population as an assault on their social and religious institutions.[24]

Lauren Monroe's recent monograph *Josiah's Reform and the Dynamics of Defilement* provides important insights into this process.[25] Monroe devotes special attention to 2 Kings 23 and persuasively identifies an original stratum therein that has far more in common with the Holiness School of the Jerusalem temple priesthood than with texts identified as Deuteronomistic.[26] According to Monroe, the Deuteronomistic passages in 2 Kings 23 are secondary additions emerging from a revision of the original, Holiness-styled pre-exilic account.[27] These secondary additions facilitated the account's inclusion in the Deuteronomistic History *en masse* and which presented Josiah as an advocate of the Deuteronomic law (2 Kgs 22:8–11; 23:1–3ff.).[28] The original, pre-exilic Holiness stratum, however, provided an account of Josiah's centralization far more in line with what one would expect from a king bent on consolidating power through sacral justification. As Monroe notes, this account lacks any real points of contact with what we encounter in Deuteronomy, and that Deuteronomy should therefore not be connected to Josiah's centralization efforts.[29] Such a connection, Monroe suggests, is strictly the result of the secondary redaction of 2 Kings 23 into the Deuteronomistic History—in her view, an exilic enterprise.

Nevertheless, even if the presentation of Deuteronomy as the motivation for Josiah's reform is a literary contrivance, this does not mean that Deuteronomy's emergence in the Josianic era is entirely a literary fiction. Just as the Deuteronomists of Monroe's model reshaped the purpose and meaning of Josiah's historical centralization efforts, so too did they reshape the purpose and meaning of Deuteronomy's actual origins in the pre-exilic period.[30] Van der Toorn has observed that Deuteronomy 12 is retrospective, drawing from royal edicts but working them into a larger literary structure which only later (during the exilic period) came to include a concern with kingship and alternate forms of leadership.[31] A similar view has been proposed by Juha Pakkala, who argues that Deuteronomy's limitations on kingship and idealized vision of Israelite social institutions could only originate at a temporal distance from the Josianic period and not, as is so often assumed, as a product of Josiah's court.[32] Though I share Pakkala's view that Deuteronomy is not a royal Josianic edict, I would suggest that it need not be post-monarchic or even post-Josianic. In fact, contra Monroe's view that Deuteronomy has no genetic connection to Josiah's reign, I would suggest the opposite: it is deeply connected to that king's activity, but not because Josiah sponsored its composition. Rather, it seems more likely that Deuteronomy surfaced in the wake of Josiah's centralization as a response to it, obtaining initially in the year 622 BCE (following the date indicated in 2 Kgs 22:3) and expanded/updated in the latter years of his reign.[33]

It is important to note that Deuteronomy's advocacy of cult centralization (chapter 12) only appears after a lengthy discourse where law and covenant are established as public trusts (chapters 5–11). The law requiring cult centralization is thereby nested within a discourse that presents it as part of an ideology emphasizing life in the land rather than setting it apart as a royal imperative of a higher order. By legitimizing centralization but affirming rural, populist covenantal concepts, Deuteronomy manages to create a textual space where royal and rural life could negotiate a tenable co-existence. Such logic undergirds other passages in Deuteronomy, such as the public appointment of regional jurists, but the depiction of those juridical agents uses terms traditionally associated with royal administration in antiquity (*šophetim we-šoterim* in Deut 16:18–20).[34] So, too, the relegation of authority to non-monarchic typologies (Deut 16:18–18:22) while placing the law of the king *directly* in the center of the unit (17:14–20) delineating these duties: the contents of each section empower rural and sacral leaders, but the form still suggests the centrality of the monarch.[35] Finally, Deuteronomy's use of rhetorical forms found in official Assyrian documents places it within reach of the royal court that interfaced with Assyrian imperial administrators,[36] but Deuteronomy's authors make the common Israelite directly accountable to YHWH as suzerain overlord, sidestepping the apparatus of the monarchy altogether.

The Deuteronomistic scenario in 2 Kings 22 supports this interest in mediation, as the narrative presents Deuteronomy as a law book discovered in the royal temple by royal agents, but read and ratified well beyond the temple precincts in the *mišneh* (loosely translated, "suburb") i.e., in the public sphere (2 Kgs 22:14). The account in 2 Kings 22 follows an ancient literary genre of "book finding," but even this diverges from the conventional use of the genre.[37] Elsewhere, the motif is used to justify royal imperatives through identifying them with the discovered book kept in an esoteric context, but in 2 Kings 22, it is used to legitimize a text made available to the public. The account is a narrative parallel to Deuteronomy's own mediating interests and has much in common with the placing of the law—usually restricted to elite priestly scribal circles—in the hands of the public (Deut 6:5–9; 11:20; 30:11–14). Like Deuteronomy, 2 Kings 22 provides a hermeneutical bridge between the popular and royal sectors, and transforms the reform account in 2 Kings 23 into an episode where Josiah champions a legal and covenantal ideology (ostensibly) rooted in populism.

While these texts may have been conceived as theoretical discourses, it does not strike me as a purely utopian vision only constructed during a post-monarchic period. Mediation between rural and royal spheres was perhaps conceived to be conceptually programmatic both in the time following Josiah's reform and then, again, in the turbulent years following Josiah's death. I would thus suggest that one dimension of Monroe's model be adjusted: the Deuteronomistic redaction of Josiah's centralization account need not be post-monarchic but, rather, need only be post-Josianic, and could derive from the same Levite scribal group that composed Deuteronomy, i.e., the Deuteronomists. It is therefore not necessary to posit an ideological clash between Deuteronomy and the Deuteronomistic History. Both exhibit Levitical and prophetic sensitivities, both share terminological and rhetorical features, and both mediate between royal and rural spheres.[38] This view is in substantial agreement with the proposal of Jeffrey C. Geoghegan, who saw the pre-exilic Deuteronomistic History emerging ca. 605–604 BCE as a platform for sustaining an increasingly fragmenting Judahite society.[39] Geoghegan's proposal is especially helpful, as he notes that the purpose of the Deuteronomists was not only to mediate between groups but between the narrative and sacral traditions they preserved.[40] In this, he accounts for contradicting sources embedded in the historiographic works he surveys that create unity by preserving and respecting diversity under a transcendent national ideology.

However, I would qualify one of Geoghegan's suppositions regarding what actually comprised this pre-exilic Deuteronomistic History, since his model presumes a single work spanning Deuteronomy–Kings. It may be more helpful to conceive of a Deuteronomistic collection of historiographic texts in the late pre-exilic period: we may identify Deuteronomistic redaction in a text without that text having to be part of a single extensive narrative such as the one Geoghegan posits. Though strong evidence points to a unified Samuel–Kings corpus already in the late pre-exilic period,[41] a number of scholars have noted that certain books often associated with the Deuteronomistic History could be better associated with a Hexateuch (such as the book of Joshua) or appear to serve as a pivot between largely independent narrative units (such as the book of Judges) and show signs of significantly later redaction.[42] This means that Joshua and Judges were still viewed as sufficiently fluid and independent to warrant such important roles in entirely different narrative complexes. Yet it is difficult to deny that certain intertextual elements in these works look ahead to Samuel–Kings or look back to Deuteronomy in a specifically Deuteronomistic manner.[43]

In sum

The Deuteronomists constructed both a legal collection (Deuteronomy) and a theoretical narrative model of Israel's landed experience (the Deuteronomistic History) for the purpose of establishing a vision of society where sacral leadership and old covenantal ideals formed the basis for evaluating righteousness, theological fidelity, and social responsibility. The ultimate (or penultimate) form of these works emerged during the period of the Babylonian Exile, but a substantial amount of narrative and legal composition took place during the last few decades of the Judahite monarchy. In this earlier phase of composition, it is likely that diverse literary collections were shaped to reflect the Deuteronomists' system of religious and social values, for the purpose of addressing forces that were dissolving Israel's surviving sense of national identity.

We may speak of Deuteronomistic redaction in Samuel–Kings *and* in other scrolls containing the traditions regarding Joshua and the Judges, establishing a theological discourse across these corpora. To explore the narratives involving Samuel, it will be essential to bear in mind that the Deuteronomistic shaping of those narratives function with intertextual simultaneity. They not only advance the ideological trajectory of Samuel–Kings, but also provide a sounding board for the consideration of other free-standing narratives worked into the Deuteronomistic History in the exilic period or later. Samuel thus functions within a work that was not always a single narrative, but which was always part of a textual curriculum with an interconnected vision. His diverse roles as priest, prophet, and judge are the end result of careful hermeneutical creativity on the part of the redactors who recognized Samuel's liminality and its potential as an interface between traditions. The point of departure, though, remains the oldest of these traditions that present Samuel as a luminary of Israel's priesthood—and in particular, as a Levite. It is within this tradition that the basis for his liminality is established, and we must therefore begin with an examination of this role in its institutional setting.

2

Samuel as a Levite

> One must put up barriers to keep one's self intact.
> —Rush, "Limelight"

According to the Chronicler, whose detailed genealogies derive from the mid-to-late 4th century BCE, Samuel was part of the ancient Levite lineage of Kohath (1 Chr 6:18–23). In the Chronicler's view, the Levitical singer Heman was a grandson of Samuel, whose own ancestors are then recounted in an extended list. The genealogy, in part, corresponds to the Chronicler's source text in 1 Samuel 1:1, where Samuel's lineage is provided in detail, beginning with his father Elkanah and extending back several generations. However, in 1 Samuel 1:1, there is no overt indication that Samuel descends from the tribe of Levi. Rather, that text states that Samuel's oldest ancestor, Zuph, is an *'ephrati*—often read/translated as "Ephraimite". For many, this poses a problem for accepting Samuel's Levitical status, since the text implies that he is associated with the tribe of Ephraim and not that of Levi.[1]

In addition, it is generally acknowledged that the Chronicler's rendition of the past is conditioned by a hermeneutical interest,[2] and this is the case with his depiction of Samuel in other contexts as well. 1 Chronicles 9:22 places Samuel on par with David in the planning of the Jerusalem temple ranks that extended into the Chronicler's own time. As most historians recognize, this is an untenable reconstruction of actual events, as the temple was a product of Solomon's reign; if David ever intended to build a temple, these intentions were never realized.³ The Chronicler may be drawing from the notice in 1 Samuel 10:25 that Samuel composed the "law(s) of the monarchy," and interpreted this verse in light of his desire to ground the Jerusalem temple and its surrounding society in Davidic initiative.⁴ But even if Samuel did establish a foundational ideology regarding the place of cultic figures in the monarchy, this would have differed tremendously from the internal mechanisms of the Jerusalem temple cult, which began as a royal institution and which was eventually assimilated into the Persian imperial superstructure of the Chronicler's day.⁵

Similar problems regarding Samuel surface in other places within the Chronicler's work. 1 Chronicles 26:28 groups Samuel with other notable pre-temple figures in the book of Samuel whose military spoils are committed to particular Levite temple families,⁶ 1 Chronicles 29:29 credits Samuel as a scribal historian, and 2 Chronicles 35:18 compares Josiah's Passover to standards begun by Samuel.⁷ In none of these cases is there additional textual evidence to support their contents. The artifice of the aforementioned passages in Chronicles requires that the genealogical details concerning Samuel be approached very cautiously.⁸ The form of the genealogy demands this as well: 1 Chronicles 6:18–23 lists several individuals named Elkanah, which suggests that the name was a device used for artificial structuring purposes rather than reflecting an authentic lineage. For this reason, many scholars are hesitant to see Samuel as a Levite, and instead view his ritual responsibilities in the narratives of 1 Samuel as a function of his prophetic authority.⁹

However, even if the specifics of the Chronicler's reconstruction are historically unreliable, the tradition of Samuel as a Levite may have been something that the Chronicler inherited and which in turn motivated his compositional decisions. Though 1 Chronicles 6:18–24 is an admixture of lineage records, it demonstrates that the Chronicler believed that Samuel was fit for inclusion into a well-known Levitical lineage. It is precisely because the Chronicler ascribes to Samuel the status of a Levite that we must consider the possibility that the Chronicler read his sources in a way that presupposed Samuel's Levite roots. And indeed, a close reading of the texts depicting Samuel's origin narrative, 1 Samuel 1–3, belies just such a connection between Samuel and the Levite priesthood. Before considering these texts, however, we must determine who exactly the Levites were, what their sacerdotal duties entailed, and how the terms "Levite" and "priest" differ.

Defining Levite status

According to the aggregate biblical tradition, the Levites are descendants of Jacob's son Levi (Gen 29:34), set aside for priestly service (Exod 32:26–9) and charged with conducting rituals, teaching divine law, sacrifice, etc. (Deut 33:8–11).[10] The Pentateuch usually qualifies the Levites as a tribe through the terms *šebet/matteh*, that is, through the monikers of kinship used for the other Israelite tribes as well, and the detailed genealogies for Levites in the Hebrew Bible leave the impression that they constituted a tribal entity. For this reason, some scholars see the Levites as an actual tribe that somehow emerged as the bearers of sacerdotal responsibility.[11] Within the Pentateuch, the Levites are further divided: Aaron and his sons are consecrated for priestly responsibilities of a higher order (Exod 28; Lev 8), and a particular Aaronide clan, the Zadokites, eventually take on the status of chief priests in Jerusalem elsewhere in the biblical record (1 Kgs 2:35; 4:4 [but cf. 1 Kgs 2:26]; Ezek 44:15). On the face of things, then, priesthood is a matter of tribal heritage and organization, and the genealogical overlaps in Exodus, Numbers, Chronicles, and elsewhere suggest an impulse toward endogamy within the Levite ranks—a feature prevalent in ancient Israelite tribal society.[12]

However, a more complicated picture of Levite origins and socio-religious function emerges when the textual sources are qualified by archaeological, anthropological, and linguistic criteria. Many scholars have accepted that the term "Levite" (Hebrew *lewi*) was not originally the proper name of an ancestor but, rather, a description of social location or function related to priestly service. Hebrew *lewi* is derived from the root *lwh*, "to attach" or "to be attached", i.e., to be placed into a client status under a patron group or individual.[13] For this reason, A. H. G. Gunneweg argued that the Levites were not a "tribe," but a caste drawn from various quarters of the Israelite population connected to priestly institutions.[14] For some researchers, the emergence of Levites as a sacral client class was facilitated with the shift to monarchy. From this perspective, Levites were individuals appointed to official priestly positions, thus "connected" to the institutions of the state cult.[15] However, even if the growth of monarchic state(s) in Israel did play a role in the establishment of some Levite groups, these royal institutions likely built upon antecedent structures. Lawrence Stager has suggested that the term *lewi* relates to the bequeathing of children to sanctuary service as a response to population growth in the Iron I period and the resulting diminishing prospects for inheritance within families of the hinterland.[16] If so, the growth of the Levite caste is decidedly pre-monarchic in origin.

Stager's view has recently been supported by the research of Jeremy Hutton. Hutton compares the record of Levite cities in Chronicles and Joshua to the function of saintly lodges among tribal populations in Morocco.[17] The priest–saint clans therein take new "initiates" into the sainthood. Some members of these clans leave the parent lodge and begin new saintly lodges in adjacent territories based on the numinous status carried over from the parent lodge. The priests–saints at these new lodges periodically claim closer genealogical connection to the ancestor believed to have founded the parent lodge, usually as a bid for the devotion of the local population. As a result, their inherited numinous authority allows them to function as interlocutors between rival socio-economic groups, adjudicators of disputes, and administrators of religious rituals that resolved conflict and established new socio-sacral structures.

Hutton also notes that priest–saint status was not necessarily permanent. Initiates could lose their saintly status if they no longer maintained the confidence of the local populations, and other saintly individuals or lineages could replace them aided by claims of close descent from an earlier and authoritative patron saint. By the same token, similar claims could be made as demoted saints or saintly groups were eventually restored to power, leading to overlapping and contradictory genealogical details shared between disparate clans.[18]

The anthropological evidence marshaled by Hutton sheds much light on texts associated with the formation of Israel's priesthood, explaining not only the overlapping and conflicting priestly genealogies in the Hebrew Bible, but also the *realia* behind the lists of Levitical cities in Joshua.[19] It also provides a plausible background to how the Levites came to be tribalized over time: once-independent priestly–saintly groups grew through expansion into new territories, creating pan-saintly kinship networks that, in turn, drew from the local populations as new initiates were taken into their ranks.[20] The apparatus of monarchic statehood over many generations invariably brought diverse ranks of Levites into contact through the affairs of state. It is reasonable to see a quasi-tribal classification either adopted by the Levite groups as they countenanced each other or, perhaps, foisted upon them by the monarchic administration as royal hierarchies asserted themselves over older tribal networks and allegiances.[21]

The foregoing leads to some important observations regarding the Levites. At least in the pre-monarchic period (and probably continuing down into the monarchic era as well) they were individuals connected to established priest–saint clans at regional sanctuaries. Once attached to these groups, they were amalgamated into their ranks and periodically struck out on their own to initiate their own priestly clans in other locations (e.g., Judg 17:7–18:31) or rose up to replace the dominant clan when its legitimacy was somehow compromised. Though a successful Levite's descendants could eventually utilize claims to biological lineage as a manner of asserting priestly power, the hallmark of Levite identity was primarily a matter of socio-religious function rather than biological lineage.

The ancient poem in Deuteronomy 33:8–11 seems to reflect this very dynamic when it describes a Levite as one who turns away from his nuclear family and devotes himself exclusively to divine service:[22]

> Thy Thummim and Thy Urim be with thy holy one[23]
> Whom thou didst prove at Massah
> With whom thou didst strive at the waters of Meribah;
> Who said of his father, and of his mother: 'I have not seen him';
> Neither did he acknowledge his brethren, nor knew he his own children;
> For they have observed thy word, and keep thy covenant.
> They shall teach Jacob thine ordinances, and Israel thy law;
> They shall put incense before thee, and whole burnt-offering upon thine altar.
> Bless, YHWH, his substance, and accept the work of his hands;
> Smite through the loins of them that rise up against him,
> And of them that hate him, that they rise not again.

In this passage, the poet has provided a model for an individual's assimilation into the Levite ranks. The Levite is to sever ties with his kinship network, devote himself exclusively to YHWH, and, as such, represent the deity in matters of adjudication, sacral instruction, and holy war (perhaps expressed in ritual terms). Nevertheless, poetic ideals do not necessarily translate into practical parallels. If Levite groups were initially bound to local populations, then the limited geographic and demographic scope of their influence would keep them in some degree of contact with their biological relatives who frequented the sanctuaries where they carried out their duties. In this case, the content of Deut 33:9 regarding the severing of kinship ties may have been regarded as a mantra of sorts for supporting ideologies that transcended kinship allegiances. Levite status was therefore inherently liminal: Levites stood between biological lineages and the priestly clans that assimilated them.

While Stager is certainly correct to identify the bequeathing of Levites to priestly clans as a measure to counter the lack of heritable resources,[24] such an act also carries a social/ethical undercurrent. Israel's social organization was formed in contra-distinction to the religious and political hierarchies of the Late Bronze Age Egypto-Canaanite culture of the lowlands, where cult and royal administration were intertwined and the peasant caste occupied a subordinate social position.[25] An Israelite allergy to these cultic hierarchies would invariably accompany the development of the nascent Israelite theology and its cult,[26] and a new standard of priestly function required the divestiture of any connection to those of the earlier types.

The relationship between pre-Israelite priestly status and royal administration is affirmed indirectly in the Hebrew Bible. The biblical authors nod several times to the close connection between priestly and royal status (1 Sam 14:35; 2 Sam 8:18; 1 Kgs 12:31; Amos 7:12), implying the fine line separating the two and the possibility that sacral authority could be parlayed into royal authority, bringing with it the potential abuse of power. In at least one case—the Gideon/Abimelekh narrative in Judges 8–9—this seems to have been the case: Gideon manages to assume priestly authority which his son, Abimelekh ("My father [is] king"), uses as the basis for his own attempt at royal rule. By contrast, the drawing of Levites from the local populations could function as a safeguard against this, with the dedication of individuals from those populations keeping the sanctuary cults rooted in an agrarian ideology.

The agrarian motif in Levitical tradition

Some telling proof-texts fleshing out this aspect of Levite function can be found in the book of Hosea. Stephen Cook's recent study of Hosea's oracles reveals that Hosea critiqued the northern culture of the 8th century BCE from the perspective of a Levite priest with an agrarian interest.[27] As Cook's study indicates, Levites served as the trustees of the divine covenant with YHWH that preserves the agrarian values of the rural population, and Hosea's oracles constantly return to agrarian imagery in delineating the terms of the relationship between Israel and their deity, as evident in the following passage:

> Therefore, behold, I will allure her, and bring her into the wilderness and speak tenderly unto her. And I will give her there her vineyards... and she shall respond there, as in the days of her youth, and as in the day when she came up out of the land of Egypt... And it shall come to pass in that day, I will respond, says YHWH, I will respond to the heavens, and they shall respond to the earth; And the earth shall respond to the corn, and the wine, and the oil.... (Hos 2:16–17, 23–4)

The prophet recalls Israel's early days when YHWH and his people enjoyed a close relationship, and the image of a wilderness that blossoms into a fertile vineyard and fields that yield corn, grapes for wine, and olives for oil is the physical metaphor for the fruitful relationship between deity and nation. While Hosea's reference to a "wilderness" may appear to recall the wilderness wandering traditions of the Pentateuch,[28] a different nuance to the oracle surfaces if he refers instead to the condition of the land before its taming by Israel's pioneer ancestors. Canaanite myth uses the term "wilderness" (*mdbr*) to describe the untamed frontier—not specifically a desert—in which the warrior deities of their pantheon do battle against cosmic foes, and set in opposition to the scenarios of the cultivated, fertile homestead where the divine family resided.[29]

This mythic concept survived in a modified form in early Israelite religion but was applied by the settlers of the highlands to their new environs, and this same concept informs Hosea's rhetoric throughout his oracles. Hosea's words do not preserve the perspective of a priest concerned with the esoteric depth of a temple or sanctuary or the cosmic implications of hermetic rituals. Rather, they reveal a consciousness deeply rooted in agrarian life, and similar examples of this modality of thought may be identified in earlier and later sources as well. Sometime in the late 7th century BCE, the prophet Jeremiah composed the following oracle as part of a critique of the religious and social shortcomings he perceived in the surrounding society:

Go, and cry in the ears of Jerusalem, saying: Thus says YHWH: I remember the affection of your youth, the love of your espousals; how you went after me in the wilderness, in a land that was not sown. Israel is YHWH's hallowed portion, his first-fruits of the increase; all that devour him shall be held guilty, evil shall come upon them, says YHWH. (Jer 2:2–3)

Like the aforementioned oracle by Hosea, this passage from the book of Jeremiah is often read against the tradition of the Pentateuchal tales of Israel wandering through the desert wilderness en route to Canaan, but it may just as easily be applied to the conditions of life early Israel faced while carving out a tenable existence in the highland frontier. This hinterland setting is even more likely when the thematic balance between "a land that was not sown" in Jeremiah 2:2 and the opening imagery of the following verse, where YHWH sets aside Israel as the "first fruits", the issuance of the land dedicated for ritual purposes.[30] Jeremiah 2:2–3 uses the language of harvest, land-tenure, and the inviolable sanctity of both. The prophet alludes to ancient conditions to invoke an ideal relationship that might be recovered if the nation believes and behaves properly.

Both Hosea and Jeremiah seem to draw from a font of tradition attested in the ancient Song of Moses currently situated in the book of Deuteronomy and which is a major source of Levite liturgical thought:[31]

For the portion of YHWH is his people; Jacob, the lot of his inheritance... he found him in a wild land... he made him ride on the high places of the land, and he did eat the fruitage of the field; and he made him suck honey out of the crag, and oil out of the flinty rock; Curd of kine, and milk of sheep, with fat of lambs, and rams of the breed of Bashan, and he-goats, with the kidney-fat of wheat; and of the blood of the grape you drank foaming wine. (Deut 32:9–10, 13–14)

Scholars have long noted the similarities between Jeremiah, Hosea, and the Song of Moses based on the recurring language and imagery shared by these texts.³² But more significant is the recurring purpose of this imagery. These texts, representing several centuries of composition, are all concerned with the pristine conditions of Israel's relationship with YHWH that are continually binding regardless of date or circumstance,³³ and this relationship is consistently one that occurs in a rural setting. In the Song of Moses, as in Hosea and Jeremiah, the poet recounts that Israel encountered YHWH while working wild, untilled soil; here, the poet specifies that this was in the highlands ("the high places of the land"). The poet then goes on to relate that Israel managed to derive sustenance against all odds by working this difficult terrain as a sort of act of devotion and with recognition that this was the will of the deity. For this devotion, YHWH provided a reward to the people by having the land yield its bounty.

This is precisely the type of value system that Levites would have espoused if their brand of sacerdotal service remained strongly informed by the needs of the lay population bound to ancestral land granted to them by YHWH. The agrarian worldviews of these families were liturgized into hymns and prayers in the early Israelite cult conducted by the Levites, whose presence maintained a check on the potential for misguided priestly authority at the local sanctuaries. Levites eventually developed a self-perception of kinship increasingly more remote from rural lay populations, but their value system remained rooted in an agrarian ideology.

Despite the interest in common agrarian values, Levites functioned as conduits between ordinary existence and the divine realm in Israelite mythic thought. It is significant that the lists of Levitical cities in Joshua position these settlements on the cusp between sedentary and transhumant social groups.³⁴ Geographically, they occupy a sort of nether region, a no-man's-land representing the mythic wilderness where the agents of chaos roamed and where the warrior deity YHWH demonstrated his power by bringing them under his control.³⁵ From this perch, occupying the space between settled territories, Levites mediated between the two worlds and functioned as representatives of the divine warrior to the populations they served.

Through their orchestration of the cult and maintenance of social order, the Levites affirmed the dominion of the warrior deity over the sacred landscape, purging chaos from its midst and keeping destructive forces at bay. As Joel Baden has argued, the origins of the Levites are remembered in different biblical sources as rooted in violent conflict and bloodshed;[36] this may be a remnant of the mythic status of Levites as foot-soldiers of YHWH. The reference to a Levite girding his loins with the sword in Deuteronomy 33:11 further resonates with this mythic model, suggesting that Levites saw their activity as a form of battle against YHWH's own cosmic foes that might somehow infect and corrode the social fabric of Israelite communities. To abrogate this responsibility was to deny the theology of YHWH as the divine warrior fighting on behalf of his people, and to invite chaos and disorder into Israelite life as a result.

Bearing all of this in mind, we shall examine Samuel's "origin narrative" in 1 Samuel 1–3 as a repository of Levitical thought and praxis.[37] Most scholars have observed features in this narrative that strongly point to its purpose with respect to the rise of Saul, especially the wordplay on the term *ša'ul* speckled throughout the first two chapters of the unit.[38] A connection between this material and the narratives introducing Saul (1 Sam 9:1–10:16; 10:17–27; 11) is undeniable, and it is indeed very likely that traditions regarding Saul have been merged with those regarding Samuel.[39] However, there are reasons to see the initial purpose in 1 Samuel 1–3 as explaining how Samuel was able to eclipse the Elides, the ruling priestly family at the Shiloh sanctuary.[40] The connection to Saul pervades the present form of the unit (especially in its larger literary context), but arises from secondary redaction or reformulation.[41]

Central to understanding the purpose of the earliest tradition in 1 Samuel 1–3 is the parallel established between Samuel and Moses. In the introduction to this study, we saw that both characters are remembered in the biblical tradition as liminal and thus capable of occupying many roles, and the appearance of a Moses/Samuel equation in other brief sources (Jer 15:1; Ps 99:6) indicates that this parallel was widely recognized. Yet as researchers have long noted, Moses is viewed as the ancestor of the Elides,[42] the very family that Samuel displaces. In 1 Samuel 1–3, we obtain a glimpse into the mechanism that stands behind this parallel and its implications for the fate of the Elide line. We will see that the Moses/Samuel parallel is deeply rooted in the understanding of Levites in relation to priestly clans discussed above, especially with regard to the role Levites played in safeguarding against the abuse of priestly power.

Samuel's origin narrative (1 Sam 1-3)

The question of proper priestly conduct and the role of Levites in assuring its standards is deeply woven into 1 Samuel 1-2. Samuel is devoted to priestly service from a regional family who continually cast their allegiance to the Shiloh sanctuary (1 Sam 1:3) and with whom Samuel maintains close contact during his priestly training (1 Sam 2:11, 18-20). Running parallel to this are the details concerning the foibles of Eli (1 Sam 1:13-14) and the corruption of his sons (1 Sam 2:12-17), who abuse their power to the detriment of public sacral interest. The "manner of the priests" related in 1 Samuel 2:13-17 may reveal the sins of the sons, but Eli's lack of punitive action (vv. 22-5) lays bare the sins of the father: he is quick to castigate the commoner Hannah (1 Sam 1:12-14), but his permissiveness regarding his sons suggests elitist entitlement. Indeed, the narrative is clear that Eli presides over the cult at Shiloh from his "throne" (*kisseh*) in 1 Samuel 1:9 and 4:13, 18, implying a dangerously close proximity between priestly and royal status.[43] It is clear from these passages that despite their formidable priestly influence, the Elides have behaved in a manner that ignores the needs and values of the public to which they were accountable. These emphases are not segregated into independent literary scenes (e.g., 1 Sam 1 dealing solely with Elkanah/Hannah; 1 Sam 2 dealing solely with the Elides), but intertwine to suggest that priestly conduct cannot be extracted from the hinterland family social context that gave rise to it.[44]

That 1 Samuel 1-2 relates to the ethics of agrarian kinship is reinforced by the oracle delivered by the anonymous prophet in 1 Samuel 2:27-36. This speech is deeply indebted to the hands of the Deuteronomists, but it preserves earlier details that shed light on the perception of Elides corruption over against more auspicious priestly ideals. The first few verses of the speech are especially revealing:

Thus says YHWH: I indeed revealed myself to the house of your father (*bet 'abikha*) when they were in Egypt in bondage to Pharaoh's house. I chose them out of all the tribes of Israel to be my priests, to ascend my altar, to burn incense, to wear an ephod before me.[45] And I gave to the house of your father (*bet 'abikha*) all the offerings of the children of Israel made by fire. Why then do you kick at my sacrifice and at my offering, which I have commanded in my habitation, and honor your sons above me, to make yourselves fat with the choicest of all the offerings of my people Israel? (1 Sam 2:27–9)

In these verses, the anonymous prophet identifies the root of Eli's complacency regarding his sons' misconduct—their claim of descent from an auspicious ancestor who served the interests of the public. Though the text is not explicit in identifying this ancestor, it appears to be Moses who is intended.[46] That the oracle heaves criticism upon the Elides by highlighting the difference between them and their ancestor suggests that it was conceived to counter an Elide claim to power based upon this genealogical connection. Claims to authority are often grounded in the rhetorical shaping of lineage details, a phenomenon surfacing in comparative anthropological models as well.[47] The twice-mentioned *bet 'abikha* identifies this as the pivotal issue in the critique, referring not only to the ancestor in question, but to the language and concept of lineage (namely, the "ancestral house," Hebrew *bet 'ab*) through which Israelite social order was broadly structured.[48] The oracle thereby impugns the genealogical basis for Elide legitimacy. As 1 Samuel 2:29 makes clear, their Mushite ancestry was an insufficient priestly qualification.[49]

As the oracle continues, the abstraction and reapplication of Mosaic language becomes especially pointed:

And I will raise up for myself a faithful priest (*kohen ne'eman*)... and I will build him a sure house (*bayit ne'eman*).... (1 Sam 2:35aα, bα)[50]

Embedded in this passage is an echo of the tradition currently found in Numbers 12:7 that identifies the unique qualities of Moses in comparison to other sacral types:

Not so with my servant Moses; he is trusted (*ne'eman*) in all my house (*beti*)...

Once again, the oracle highlights the gulf between the Elides and Moses, going so far as to say that a non-Elide (a priest of a different "house") will inherit Mosaic qualities. In this case, the rhetoric of the oracle deflates the efficacy of the Elide strategy: laying claim to the traditions of their ancestor Moses is futile, for a non-Elide will be characterized by those Mosaic traits irrespective of biological descent according to YHWH's will.

1 Samuel 2:27–36 is overtly retrospective. It knows not only that Eli's sons will die, but that the surviving Elides will be demoted to a client status (v. 36). This could support a Deuteronomistic provenance for the entire oracle in relation to the house of Zadok, replacing the Elides at Solomon's ascent to the throne (1 Kgs 2:26–7). However, its use of Mosaic rhetoric means that it also knows that the "faithful priest" who replaced the Elides was regarded as Mosaic in typology, a quality that is nowhere else applied to Zadok, the Zadokites, or the Aaronides more generally.[51] The original form of the oracle thus relates to a different challenger to Elide priestly dominance, and Samuel stands out as the prime candidate given the ensuing events in 1 Samuel. The retrospective content of the oracle points to its origins among a group that adopted Samuel as their founder or patron, characterizing the rise of their scion as divinely mandated over against the priestly clan to which he was entrusted.

Here, however, we encounter a potential problem: according to both textual and anthropological evidence, a Levite derives sacral authority through the numinous power of the priests under whom he received training.[52] Yet it is clear from 1 Samuel 1–2 that the Elides are no saints in terms of their commitment to public welfare or connection to the realm of the divine. In effect, Samuel's priestly training under the Elides is a potential liability.[53] That the narrative places Samuel under Elide tutelage weighs in favor of a genuine historical connection between Samuel and the Elides at Shiloh. A pro-Samuel tradent conceiving a free composition would hardly fashion a narrative so heavily critical of the Elides on the one hand and then depict Samuel's priestly enculturation under that same flawed family on the other; the narrative must therefore reflect the memory of Samuel's actual training at Shiloh.[54] But in order for Samuel to supersede the Elides and claim the mantle of Mosaic leadership, a new encounter with the divine was needed to authenticate his leadership as sufficiently numinous, and one that could rival—and sideline—the Elides' genealogical claims of descent from Moses.

The narrative of 1 Samuel 3 provides the details regarding just such an encounter. In this episode, Samuel moves from priestly adept to prophet via his nighttime encounter with YHWH in the crypt containing the Ark, where YHWH informs him that the Elides will be punished for their abuse of power (vv. 11–14).[55] Many scholars have

Samuel as a Levite 35

argued that 1 Samuel 3 is an account of a dream theophany.[56] This view is understandable, since revelation in the dream state is a common fixture of ancient prophecy. Moreover, as C. L. Seow has demonstrated, the Shiloh sanctuary fostered remnants of an old El cult, and the Ugaritic literature is clear that El often makes his will known through dreams.[57] Given this setting, and taking into consideration the El theophoric in both Samuel's own name and that of his father (*šemu'el*; *'elqanah*), it is reasonable to conclude that the narrative presents the contents of the divine revelation as a dream vision concomitant with the predilections of the El traditions. However, a closer look at the events within the episode suggests a different set of circumstances:

And YHWH called [to] Samuel;[58] and he said: 'Here am I (*hinneni*).' And he ran to Eli, and said: 'Here am I; for you called me.' And he said: 'I called not; lie down again.' And he went and lay down. And YHWH called Samuel yet again. And Samuel arose and went to Eli, and said: 'Here am I; for you called me.' And he answered: 'I called not, my son; lie down again.' Now Samuel did not yet know YHWH, and the word of YHWH (*dabar YHWH*) was not yet revealed to him. And YHWH called Samuel again a third time. And he arose and went to Eli, and said: 'Here am I; for you called me.' And Eli perceived that YHWH was calling the child. Therefore Eli said to Samuel: 'Go, lie down; and it shall be, if you are called, that you will say: Speak, YHWH; for your servant (*'abdekha*) hears.' So Samuel went and lay down in his place. And YHWH came, and stood (*wayyabo' YHWH wayyityatzeb*), and called as at other times: 'Samuel, Samuel.' Then Samuel said: 'speak; for your servant (*'abdekha*) hears.'

In this passage, the divine voice calling Samuel rouses him from his slumber; Samuel is awake as he runs to Eli in response to the voice that he hears. The implication is that just as he is awake when he runs to Eli, Samuel is awake as he finally answers YHWH's call. Robert Gnuse notes that the awakening of the dreamer is a common feature of the dream theophany, at which point the deity shows the awakened dreamer a vision.[59] However, Samuel does *not* receive a vision in 1 Samuel 3—there is no vision report offered or imagery described, only the relating of divine intention and the subsequent account of Samuel conveying the divine word to Eli (v. 18). Indeed, it is the divine word (*dabar YHWH*), not dreams or visions, which receives repeated emphasis throughout the narrative.

This reflects a phenomenology rather different than visionary experience as attested in other prophetic contexts.[60] It may be that the author, aware of the El tradition fostered at Shiloh, flavored the narrative with a setting suggestive of a dream theophany for the sake of formal authenticity.[61] But even while including the familiar elements of dream theophanies, the account deliberately draws a *distinction* between the type of dream theophany the audience might expect at the outset of the narrative and what Samuel ultimately experiences. The end result of the narrative creates distance between Samuel and the Elides, as his experience stands apart from what is presented as business-as-usual under their guidance.[62]

The unexpected turns in the narrative have much in common with the traditions about YHWH's relationship with Moses. Parallels between Samuel's encounter with YHWH and that of Moses in Exodus 3 have long been noted: both receive a call that repeats their name (1 Sam 3:10; Exod 3:4), both respond with *hinneni* (1 Sam 3:4–5, 8; Exod 3:4), the divine appears before both (Moses hides his face to avoid seeing the divine countenance in Exod 3:6), and Samuel will receive a revelation (*yigleh* in 3:7) akin to YHWH's earlier revelation to Moses as spoken by the anonymous prophet in the previous chapter (*nigloh nigleti* in 1 Sam 2:27).[63] However, the episode in Numbers 12 noted above is especially pertinent to the Moses/Samuel parallel. A look at the larger passage is instructive:

> Hear now my words:
> If there be a prophet among you,
> I YHWH make myself known to him in a vision,
> I speak with him in a dream.
> Not so with my servant (*'abdi*) Moses;
> He is trusted in all my house;
> With him do I speak mouth to mouth (*peh 'el peh*) directly, and not in dark speeches;
> And he beholds the similitude of YHWH (*temunat YHWH*). (Num 12:6–8)

In this passage Moses is categorized as completely unique from other intermediaries: YHWH appears in person to Moses, who sees the divine presence (*temunat YHWH*) and with whom he speaks directly (*peh 'el peh*). The redactor of Numbers has drawn these verses from an ancient source (evidenced in part by their poetic structure),[64] and the antiquity of the tradition behind this source is supported not only by the passage in Exodus 3:6, but by the persistence of this same idea in different strata of the Pentateuch (Exod 33:11; Deut 34:10). Evidently, the concept of the deity speaking directly to Moses was too firmly entrenched for later biblical writers/redactors to ignore or curb, even in the face of later ideologies that had increasingly abstracted the divine presence and rendered it transcendent rather than immanent (see, e.g., Jer 23:23 [MT]). When we consider that Samuel, like Moses, is identified as YHWH's *'ebed* (v. 10), that the revelation to him is conveyed in the waking state, and that the deity literally appears before him (*wayyabo' YHWH wayyityatzeb* in v. 10), the parallels between the Moses tradition in Numbers 12:6–8 and 1 Samuel 3 become even more concrete.

In attempting to identify a social setting for the origination of Numbers 12:6–8, I would suggest that an early form of this tradition—or at least the concept behind it—obtained among the Elides in an attempt to retain priestly power after the destruction of Shiloh (ca. 1050 BCE and reflected in the narrative of 1 Sam 4). Pursuant to the El traditions that persisted at that sanctuary identified by Seow, dream theophanies are accepted as legitimate in these verses,[65] but Moses is held above those who receive them. This would support Elide claims to superiority over potential challengers to their priestly authority: descent from Moses, the man with whom YHWH spoke directly, trumps other numinous claims. This also sheds some light on why Samuel is asleep in the sacred crypt at the outset of 1 Samuel 3. If the suggestion of some commentators is correct that the young Samuel sleeps in the sacred crypt for the purpose of incubating a dream theophany,[66] then this presupposes the Elide attempt to control revelatory hierarchies.[67] It asserts that the authority of the Elides derived from their ancestors' direct encounter with YHWH, and was higher and mightier than subsidiary forms of revelation.

What eventually unfolds, however, is a rather dramatic turn of events that accomplishes two things simultaneously. First, it contributes to the sense throughout the narrative of 1 Samuel 1–3 that the standards and practices of the Elides were ineffective, dream incubation included (as suggested by the opening note *'eyn hazon niphratz*). Samuel's revelation is a unique event, something that does not occur under the aegis of Elide strategy. Second, and building upon the first, it declares that Samuel has the very same experience that is elsewhere attributed to Moses, i.e., YHWH speaking directly to him in a waking state. As we have seen, this is reinforced by the words of the anonymous prophet in 1 Samuel 2:35 who claims that the new priestly house eclipsing the Elides was to be founded by a figure who will himself carry Mosaic qualities similar to those in Numbers 12:6–8.

I have suggested elsewhere that before the Deuteronomists redacted the material currently found in 1 Samuel 1–3, much of the oracle in 1 Samuel 2:27–36 was once part of the message received by Samuel in 1 Samuel 3.[68] By placing it in the mouth of an anonymous prophet before Samuel's own experience in the crypt, 1 Samuel 2:35 is removed from any tradition of Samuel's rise to priestly power and is then applied to the removal of the Elide Abiathar and the rise of the house of Zadok under Solomon (1 Kgs 2:26–7). However, in its pre-Deuteronomistic state, the oracle likely rested within the recounting of revelation given to Samuel in the crypt, consistent as it is with the Mosaic overtones pervading 1 Samuel 3. The entire episode rendered Samuel the recipient of an unmitigated divine encounter that trumps the numinous claims of the Elides, one that follows a Mosaic paradigm and one that thereby fulfills its own prediction of a "faithful priest"—Samuel—rising up to helm the cult.

In the early Samuel narratives we thus find the origin of the Moses/Samuel parallel and the generating circumstances behind its construction. The revelation to Samuel in 1 Samuel 3 becomes the basis for an argument against the Elides that descent from Moses was enough to maintain priestly hegemony under compromised circumstances. Rather, Mosaic typology was just that—a typology of sacral status that could be granted by YHWH to a fitting substitute not bound by biological lineage to the Mushite line. This included not only the ability to communicate with the divine (a quality of which the Elides are bereft in 1 Sam 1–3), but also to maintain social order among the populace. If Moses was trusted with the entirety of the divine "house" (Num 12:8), this surely included the social structures of the hinterland that YHWH had planted therein (Exod 15:13, 17).[69]

Here the agrarian impulse mentioned above comes into play. Samuel's towering stature in subsequent chapters and his influence in the earliest days of the monarchy retained the perception that he repaired the injuries to the socio-sacral order perpetrated by the Elides. To be a faithful priest, a priest like Moses, required a commitment to hinterland life and values alongside ritual authority and oracular ability. The Samuel traditions highlight these traits alongside Samuel's oracular and priestly qualities. Elkanah's good clan-based lineage and highland residence (1 Sam 1:1), Hannah's devotion to the ethic of procreation,[70] Samuel's ongoing interaction with his family while in priestly training, and later Samuel's commitment to maintaining juridical standards throughout the hinterland all make clear that his fitness for cultic leadership was rooted in the Levitical value system that championed agrarian society.[71]

As noted above, the late 7th–early 6th century allusion to the Moses–Samuel parallel in Jeremiah 15:1 demonstrates the degree to which Samuel's Levitical status was accepted and venerated in subsequent tradition:

Then YHWH said to me: 'Though Moses and Samuel would stand before me, yet my mind could not be toward this people; cast them out of my sight, and let them go forth...'

Here, the prophet Jeremiah claims that Israel has fallen to such depths that even revered figures such as Moses and Samuel could not redeem them. A case could be made that this passage simply appeals to well-known figures from the past in order to contextualize conditions in the author's present. This may well be true, but it is important to bear in mind that Jeremiah was a Levite from the priestly village of Anatoth (Jer 1:1), the home-base of the Elide Abiathar who was exiled there from Jerusalem during the reign of Solomon (1 Kgs 2:26). Jeremiah is presented as seizing upon a non-Elide as a typological antecedent for his own activity while simultaneously invoking the name of Moses. This brief passage shows that even among the descendants of the Elides, the Samuel–Moses equation had taken root, suggesting its introduction into that priestly group's stream of tradition in a much earlier period. A time must have come where Samuel's dominance could no longer be questioned even by the Elides, and equations forged between Samuel and Moses were accepted by the Elide supporters as a matter of good political strategy if they were to continue to have any priestly power at all.

In sum

1 Samuel 1–3 function as a description of Levitical purpose. They provide a narrative schematic for the conditions under which a child was set aside for devotional service as a Levite at a major sanctuary, as well as how such a Levite could rise up to replace the dominant priestly family at that sanctuary when the family in question was no longer fit to serve the needs of the public. Samuel stands out as a pivotal figure entrusted with mediating conflicts, connecting the earthly and ethereal realms, and promoting the foundational social values embedded in Israel's early theology. The shapers of this narrative justify his fitness for assuming these awesome responsibilities by arguing that Samuel was the true inheritor of Moses' authority, even above and beyond the status of Moses' own biological descendants. This gives us some insight into the often fuzzy distinction between priests and Levites. At least in the early period, Levites could become full-blown priests by virtue of advantageous circumstances where no other priestly family was dominant in a particular area (what Hutton has termed "fission"[72]) or, as in Samuel's case, displacing an extant priestly family and proclaiming typological equivalency with their founding saintly ancestor.

It is for this reason that Levites eventually identified broadly with Moses as their symbolic patron—if Samuel's tale is taken as paradigmatic, then the typology of Moses or other saintly founders was assumed by Levite dedicants elsewhere as well as they or their supporters challenged the priestly status quo at different sanctuaries. If the Chronicler saw fit to include non-Levites into his vision of a "greater Levite" faculty, it was because the institution of Levites and priests was always permeable, with commoners becoming Levites and Levites becoming priests, as Samuel's own trek exemplifies.

3

Samuel as a Prophet

Tough times demand tough talk.
—Rush, "Force Ten"

The previous discussion of Samuel's function as a Levite explains the tale of his rise to priestly prominence at Shiloh and, subsequently, his position as the primary representative of the Levites in the days before the birth of the monarchy. At the heart of this is the prophetic experience in 1 Samuel 3, which affirms his numinous connection to YHWH and his consequent right to herald the deity to the public. It is Samuel's prophetic qualifications that stand out most prominently within the biblical tradition: the Chronicler focuses on his prophetic role far more than his Levite status, as does Jeremiah, and this role receives the majority of emphasis in the later exegetical tradition as well.[1] The move from "Levite" to "prophet" is not one of complete categorical distinction, though; as we will see below, the lines that divide the two typologies are somewhat permeable. Nevertheless, the liminal nature inherent to Samuel's role as a Levite contributed to later prophets claiming Samuel as an archetype for their own movement.

Defining and qualifying Israelite prophecy

The word "prophet" (Hebrew *nabi'*) is applied rather broadly in the biblical record and carries a range of meanings. Prophets are depicted as cultic ecstatics, visionaries, seers, liturgical singers, and mantic scribes, and many of these types see parallels in extra-biblical sources from neighboring ancient cultures.[2] However, the dominant image of Israelite prophecy is informed by the collective impact of the prophetic literary corpus (Isaiah, Jeremiah, Ezekiel, the book of the Twelve) and the narratives in the Deuteronomistic History. In these works, the prophets are the perceived spokespersons of YHWH who provide insight into the conditions that maintain Israel's covenant relationship with their patron deity. In some contexts, these prophets of YHWH are misguided in their views and evaluations, and the biblical writers sometimes identify these figures as offering oracles motivated by a spirit of falsehood (see, e.g., 1 Kgs 22) or, alternately, as delivering oracles purportedly on YHWH's behalf but later deemed incorrect (e.g., Hannaniah in Jeremiah 28). Determining who is a true prophet within the biblical canon should supposedly be fairly straightforward: a true prophet would be a figure whose words on behalf of YHWH are considered authentic and accurate.

But as research into Israelite prophecy has demonstrated time and time again, it is exceedingly difficult to identify standards for qualifying prophets as "true." Indeed, Deut 13:2–3 admits that illegitimate prophets may speak oracles that come to pass and provide portents that are authentic. On the other side of the equation, legitimate prophets may offer statements that do *not* come true. The 8th-century prophet Micah predicted the imminent destruction of Jerusalem in his own day (Mic 3:12); though this oracle did not come to fruition for well over a century after it was delivered, Micah was still accepted as an authentic prophetic voice (Jer 26:17–19). For these and other reasons, "true" vs. "false" prophecy is increasingly regarded as an untenable dichotomy.[3]

The question should be reframed as whether a particular prophet espouses concepts that, in a given social or historical context, might be perceived as authentically Yahwistic,[4] though this too is a complicated matter. No scholar would look at literary figures such as Elijah, Amos, or Isaiah and deny that each of these represents authoritative prophetic voices within the biblical tradition, but each is markedly different from the other. Elijah is a folkloristic character whose legends were worked into the book of Kings, but who left no collection of his written oracles like Amos or Isaiah.[5] And even though Amos and Isaiah are both associated with written texts bearing their respective names, the social and theological emphases within these books differ significantly.[6]

The picture is complicated further by the fact that in many cases, authentic prophets of YHWH flat-out disagree with each other. Isaiah views Jerusalem as eternally under YHWH's protection (Isaiah 29), while his contemporary Micah predicts its destruction (Mic 3:12), and whereas Hosea states that YHWH will take back his estranged "wife" Israel (Hos 3:1–5), Jeremiah implies that this is beyond possibility (Jer 3:1–5).[7] In the Deuteronomistic History, too, discrepancies emerge: prophets stand against the social power structures in some cases while serving Israel's kings as trusted counselors in others. They are on the one hand presented as the bearers of Moses' legacy as defenders of the covenant stipulations (1 Sam 2:27–36; 1 Samuel 12; 1 Kgs 11:29–39; 1 Kgs 13:1–10; etc.), while denied the opportunity to experience YHWH in a Mosaic manner on the other (1 Kgs 19).

Apart from these and other points of disagreement, there is also the inescapable fact that the canonization of texts associated with "authentic" prophets reflects choices made by a limited group of later scribes to identify only certain individuals as part of Israel's authentic prophetic legacy.[8] In some cases, the biblical record speaks approvingly but in protracted ways about other prophets about whom we have come to know very little and whose oracles or deeds are lost to history (e.g., Jer 26:20–3). In other cases, prophets that ancient audiences would have viewed as legitimate and compelling are written out of the national history in accordance with prevailing ideological trends or policies—one may imagine, for example, that the allegedly seditious prophets outlawed in Deuteronomy 13:2–7 correspond to genuine social types that the authors wished to silence.[9] And yet it is clear from passages such as Jeremiah 44:15–19 that an audience existed for these censured prophetic types, even if the biblical writers tell us virtually nothing else about them. As Blenkinsopp has observed, "those who we refer to as *the* prophets formed a small, and in some respects anomalous, minority of prophets in Israel at any given time."[10]

For the purposes of the present study, it will suffice to identify prophecy as a vehicle for expressing social values presented as divine revelation to a given individual or a limited group. In this regard, prophecy has much in common with priestly teaching, and scholars have noted that depictions of the early priesthood (such as in 1 Sam 1–3) see prophecy as a subset of priestly responsibility.[11] Yet in time, prophetic duties eventually came to be viewed as distinct from the intermediary role of priests. Evidence for this may be found in the near-contemporaneous works of Jeremiah and Ezekiel, prophets active in the early 6th century BCE:

> Then said they: 'Come, and let us devise devices against Jeremiah; for instruction (*torah*) shall not perish from the priest, nor counsel from the wise, nor the word from the prophet...'. (Jer 18:18)
>
> Disaster will come upon disaster and rumor will be added to rumor; then they will seek a vision from a prophet, but instruction (*torah*) will be lost from the priest and counsel from the elders. (Ezek 7:26)[12]

In both passages, prophets are entrusted with either the divine word or divine visions, while priests claim dominion over the teaching of divine instruction (*torah*). The content of these verses is fitting for their respective literary settings, for Ezekiel and Jeremiah both are characterized as teaching *torah* through their deliverance of prophetic oracles rather than through priestly function. These texts attest to a division of labor that had emerged by the time the writers of each work set pen to parchment, where the status of prophet was more closely associated with delivering oracles than in teaching *torah*, a form of instruction vested in the priesthood. This type of separation is already attested in Hosea's 8th-century BCE invective against the priestly establishment at the northern sanctuary of Bethel:

> My people are destroyed for lack of knowledge; because thou hast rejected knowledge, I will also reject thee, that thou shalt be no priest to me; seeing thou hast forgotten the instruction (*torah*) of thy God, I also will forget thy children. (Hos 4:6)

Hosea's interest in priestly *torah* instruction is strongly affected by his own Levitical heritage,[13] but it is significant that the critique is presented in oracular form as a divine message from YHWH. As with the aphorisms in Jeremiah and Ezekiel, Hosea's words evidence a separation of duties or imperatives between priests and prophets, and he ultimately identifies with the latter typology. Hosea 9:7 reveals that ecstatic prophecy connected to cult sites is no longer a suitable vehicles for divining YHWH's will ("the man of the spirit is insane"), while Hosea 9:8 relates that true prophecy is a matter of the prophet serving as a divine watchman over the nation ("the watchman of Ephraim is with his god" in v. 8).[14] Likewise, when Hosea recalls the Exodus, he refers to Moses' leadership in prophetic terms (Hos 12:14) and makes clear that YHWH reveals his will through prophets rather than priests (Hos 12:11).

Even if individuals like Hosea, Jeremiah, and Ezekiel possessed priestly heritage and drew inspiration from that background, their words are compelling because they function in a prophetic mode. Prophetic critique seems to have replaced the earlier practice attested within Samuel's origin narrative of a "new priest" arising from the ranks of Levites to supplant and replace a sanctuary's questionable priestly faculty. We may attribute this to the fact that in the monarchic period, priestly clans at the major sanctuaries were royally sponsored and served the interests of the royal elite (e.g., Amos 7:13).[15] If a priestly group had lost the allegiance of the rural peasants, the apparatus of the state still maintained an economic and social status quo that kept them in power. In such a sociological context, the possibility of a Levite challenging an unfit priestly family and replacing them such as we encounter in 1 Samuel 1–3 seems to be a rather remote possibility.

This provides some support for Cross's position that the premonarchic period saw prophecy subsumed within priesthood and that prophecy as an "independent" institution rose with the monarchy. With the major priestly clans supported by the state, prophetic protest replaced the older Levite safeguard against corrupt or ineffectual priests, and became the only viable means of expressing dissent concerning priestly shortcomings.[16] But this also means that prophecy—at least, the type of prophecy that critiqued the official state priesthoods—was relegated to a social status in closer proximity to the rural hinterland classes than to the socio-economic elite whose fortunes were bound to state institutions.[17] By Hosea's day, prophets had taken up the role earlier played by Levites as bearers of the old agrarian value system, mediators between the priestly establishment and the hinterland families, and deliverers of divine oracles.[18] It may be the case that some Levites who did not assimilate into the state cult shifted gears and identified as prophetic guilds over against the claims of priesthoods now rooted in the royally supported sanctuaries.[19]

It is instructive to compare this image of prophecy to the common picture of prophetic function in other ancient near eastern contexts. Though there must have been prophetic functionaries who stood outside the mainstream (and we periodically encounter prophets who are critical of the royal administration), the wealth of ancient texts from both west Semitic and Mesopotamian cultures present prophets as tightly bound to the royal sanctuaries, serving sometimes as mediators between the divine and the king and even functioning as propagandists for royal interests.[20] The Hebrew Bible preserves wisps of parallels to these foreign types of prophecy: David has his own "court" prophets (Gad and Nathan), Ahab is reported to have possessed prophetic supporters on the royal payroll (1 Kgs 22), and a number of prophets mentioned in the book of Jeremiah appear to espouse an ideology that dovetails with the interests of the kings of Jerusalem (Jer 26–9; see also above re: Jer 18:18, where prophets are part of an "insider" triad).

The book of Amos possesses an especially telling passage, Amos 7:10–17, where the prophet Amos and Amaziah, chief priest of the royal sanctuary at Bethel, engage in verbal fisticuffs. Amos proclaims that he is no "prophet's son" (*ben nabi'* in v. 14), i.e., he is no member of a professional prophetic guild akin to those linked to state sanctuaries and under royal patronage. This indicates that the norm for prophecy involved the guilds or institutions against which Amos defined himself—he is *not* what one would expect according to prophetic convention in the mid to late 8th century BCE. By and large, prophecy in Deuteronomistic narratives follows the self-perception that Amos himself articulates in Amos 7:14—it is set apart from royal patronage and divorced from the institutions of the state. It appears more often as a gauge for the folly of kings rather than as an instrument of royal power or legitimacy.[21]

All of this bears heavily upon the characterization of Samuel as a prophet in the Deuteronomistic History. Here Jeremiah 15:1 is highly significant, for it demonstrates that Jeremiah regarded Samuel first and foremost as a prophet who set the stage for his own mission in the late 7th century BCE.[22] If Jeremiah 15:1 invokes the name of Samuel alongside that of Moses, it is because the author viewed Samuel as a

Mosaic prophet of Deuteronomistic proportions. By the late 7th century, then, Samuel's prophetic status outweighed his Levite heritage in the discourse of the biblical authors. We will thus consider his role as a prophetic pivot of sorts in the Deuteronomistic History on the one hand, and his connection to the "classical" 8th-century prophets on the other.

Samuel's prophetic function in the Deuteronomistic history

Within the narrative of the Deuteronomistic History, the figure of Samuel mediates between Joshua—Judges on the one hand and Samuel—Kings on the other. The literary sinews that accomplish this are primarily a matter of smart redactional strategy; narratives in Judges, the Samuel origin narrative, and finally the narrative of Saul's rise to power all play on the lexical formula "now there was a [certain] man," a phrase that establishes semantic connections between these once independent traditions.[23] Lexical formulae such as this reveal the seams that were created to weave a larger tale, reshaping the sources in the process.

There are broader motifs that connect these works through the Samuel narratives as well in relation to cult sites and the social role they play. Samuel–Kings is largely concerned with the centrality of the Jerusalem cult sponsored by the Davidic kings, and Samuel of course inaugurates David as the ruler fit to found this cult site. However, as we have already seen, Samuel is the figure most prominently associated with the legacy of the Shiloh sanctuary, perceived in different ways as the predecessor to Jerusalem in the biblical record (Ps 99:6 [by implication];[24] Ps 78:60–8). It is no coincidence that Shiloh factors significantly into both the books of Joshua and Judges. Let us first consider an important passage from Joshua 18:

And the whole congregation of the children of Israel assembled themselves together at Shiloh, and set up the tent of meeting there; and the land was subdued before them... and Joshua charged those that went to describe the land, saying "go and walk through the land, and describe it, and come back to me, and I will cast lots for you here before YHWH in Shiloh." And the men went and passed through the land... and they came to Joshua at the camp at Shiloh. And Joshua cast lots for them in Shiloh before YHWH; and there

Joshua divided the land for the children of Israel according to their divisions. (Josh 18:1, 10)

In this passage, Shiloh functions as an administrative center for the allocation of land to the Israelite tribes under Joshua's leadership. The narrative is by no means an accurate historical account, but it preserves the cultural memory of Shiloh's pre-eminent place as a sacred site for large swathes of Israelite populations in the late 12th through mid 11th centuries BCE.[25] This much, at least, loosely resonates with genuine circumstances with one notable exception, namely, that Judah is included in this league of tribes whose land claims are determined at Shiloh. There is a scholarly consensus that the northern Israelite populations were far more developed and interconnected than Judah until at least the 10th century BCE, for it was only then that a significant settlement expansion is attested in Judahite territory.[26] Though some communities in Judah may have had limited interaction with the tribes of the north and the Shiloh sanctuary,[27] the majority of the small Judahite population conducted their religious affairs independently of the religious network based at Shiloh.

What is significant, then, about the inclusion of Judah into the account of the tribal allotments at Shiloh, and how does this relate to the Deuteronomistic concept of prophetic authority? YHWH's opening message to Joshua reveals much in this regard:

Moses my servant is dead; now therefore arise, go over this Jordan, you, and all this people, to the land which I give to them, even to the children of Israel. Every place that the sole of your foot shall tread upon, to you have I given it, as I spoke to Moses... No man shall be able to stand before you all the days of your life; as I was with Moses, so I will be with you; I will not fail you, nor forsake you... Only be strong and very courageous, *to observe to do according to all the law, which Moses my servant commanded you; turn not from it to the right hand or to the left, that you may have good success wherever you go. This book of the law shall not depart from your mouth, but you shall meditate therein day and night, that you may observe to do according to all that is written therein*; for then you shall make your ways prosperous, and then you shall have good success. (Josh 1:2–8)

The opening canto of the book of Joshua identifies the real authority figure setting the agenda for the book: Moses, the prototype of

Samuel as a Prophet 49

prophecy. The name of Moses is mentioned no less than six times in eight verses. What is especially significant is the italicized passage in vv. 7–8 identifying the *torah* of Moses as the basis for Joshua's own role as Israel's leader. As commentators have long noted, the language of these verses is extremely similar to the language of Deuteronomy 17:18–20, which legislates that an Israelite king must study the written *torah* of Moses as well, and must not veer "to the right or to the left" from what it demands in order to have a successful reign.[28]

Here is where the inclusion of Judah stands out, for Deuteronomy is a product of scribes who resided in Judah and supports a centralized cult that aligns, to some degree, with the policies of Judahite kings such as Hezekiah and Josiah.[29] And significantly, both of these kings are reported to have deferred to the authority of the prophets of their day and the divine *torah* these prophets advocated (2 Kgs 18:1–4; 22:4–20; Jer 26:17–19).[30] The connection between ruler, *torah*, and prophet is presaged by the Shiloh scenario in Joshua 18. The text intimates that the rule of the Davidic kings from Jerusalem, Judah's pre-eminent city, is meant to carry forward the authority of Joshua's leadership at Shiloh where the definitive prophetic teaching, the *torah* of Moses, was first instituted. To follow law and policy emanating from Jerusalem, then, is to reconnect with hallowed Mosaic antiquity. In Joshua 18, Joshua is simply the vehicle for Moses' prophetic authority, and Shiloh is the chosen place where this authority was to be rooted. The entire scenario is a model for an ideal royal Jerusalemite culture from the Deuteronomists' perspective.[31]

Yet by the time Shiloh makes its appearance in the book of Judges (chapter 21), the circumstances have degenerated dramatically. The major reference to the sanctuary occurs in the following passage:

And they said "behold, there is the annual feast of YHWH in Shiloh"...And they commanded the Benjaminites, saying "go and lie in wait in the vineyards; and see, and, behold, if the daughters of Shiloh come out to dance in the dances, then come out of the vineyards, and each of you catch for yourself a wife from the daughters of Shiloh"...in those days there was no king in Israel; every man did that which was right in his own eyes. (Judg 21:19–24)

The narrative in which these passages appear is often termed a "text of terror,"[32] and rightly so, for it is full of horrific events and actions signaling Israel's descent into near oblivion.[33] The tale begins with rape and, as the passage suggests, ends with rape as well (the "catching" of young women). Shiloh still appears to be a central landmark for Israel's tribal population, but not because of its place as a hub of prophecy and law. In contrast to Joshua 18, Shiloh succumbs to the lawlessness and brutality of the surrounding population as its "daughters" (probably young women engaged in a harvest festival) are kidnapped and forced into marriage with the remaining Benjaminites.[34]

A key to understanding the importance of this degenerate state is indicated earlier in the same chapter, where Shiloh is referred to as situated in "the land of Canaan" (v. 12). This has led some to see this as evidence for implied disregard for Shiloh as a major sanctuary or as standing on non-Israelite territory.[35] Indeed, as Donald Schley notes, an identical collocation ("Shiloh that is in the land of Canaan") occurs in Joshua 21:12 as part of the description of the land as it was allocated to Israel's tribes.[36] The language in Judges may very well have been conceived in conscious awareness of the language in Joshua, or vice versa, and both perhaps bear witness to the persistence of a memory of Shiloh's importance as a pre-Israelite cult site.[37]

In the context of the Judges narrative, however, an additional valence may be sensed: the reference to Shiloh in "Canaanite" territory may reflect the author's view that because prophetic authority had gone dormant, the Israelite characters of the narrative have taken a turn back to their reviled pre-Israelite cultural patrimonies. The final verse in Judges 21 suggests that kingship can function as a safeguard against such social dissolution, though we have already seen from Joshua 18 that the king is to be an executor of prophetic will. Read together, both Joshua and Judges make a strong case for the need for prophetic guidance, presenting opposing examples of what Israelite life will be like both with and without such guidance.[38]

The closing chapter of Judges presents a Shiloh sanctuary bereft of prophecy, and this is the same picture of Shiloh in the opening chapters of the book of Samuel. 1 Samuel 3:1 specifies that during Eli's tenure as chief priest, the prophetic word of YHWH was rare and oracular visions were entirely lacking. With Samuel's appearance at Shiloh, however, prophecy suddenly surfaces again, first in the anti-Elide oracle delivered by an anonymous prophet (1 Sam 2:27–36) and then again with Samuel's own prophetic experience in the sacred crypt before YHWH's Ark (1 Sam 3:3–18).[39] By the end of 1 Samuel 3, prophecy is once again in full bloom, and the once-fragmented nation we encounter at the end of the book of Judges has begun to experience a type of restoration via Samuel's prophetic abilities (1 Sam 3:20). Most significantly, Samuel's prophetic skills lead the narrator to state that "once more, YHWH appeared at Shiloh, for YHWH revealed himself to Samuel at Shiloh through the word of YHWH" (1 Sam 3:21). The literary structure of this verse demands closer attention, as it forms a chiasmus:

YHWH appeared
  at Shiloh
    For YHWH revealed himself to Samuel
  at Shiloh
through the word of YHWH

The central statement in this verse (italicized) drives home the pivotal role Samuel plays in the history of Israel. The chiasmus noted above—which occurs only in the MT version of the chapter—indicates that Samuel's role serves to rehabilitate Shiloh from its compromised state. The MT version of the chapter's conclusion may therefore be the result of a Deuteronomistic redaction of an earlier tradition.[40] Though the Samuel origin narrative was originally composed in relation to Samuel's priestly eclipse of the Elides, its current form serves as a climax, in some ways, to the history of prophecy in early Israel as related in Joshua and Judges.[41] The literary form of 1 Samuel 3:21 leaves no doubt that it is Samuel who restores Shiloh to the glory it held in Joshua's day. Since Samuel now seems to be a renewed conduit for communication with YHWH, the reader is poised to anticipate a return to circumstances at Shiloh as they obtained under Joshua, i.e., a return to the standards of *torah* bequeathed to Israel by Moses.

In the broad strokes, Samuel's prophetic function within the Deuteronomistic History parallels that of Moses: both intercede between the nation and YHWH (Deut 5:4–5; 18:16; 1 Sam 7:3–14; 12:18–23), both convey prophecy through the divine word (Deut 18:18; 1 Sam 3:22), both institute legislation regarding kingship (Deut 17:14–20; 1 Sam 10:25), and both commission "civil" leaders who are to function within the parameters of their prophetic teachings and authority (Deut 31:14, 23; Josh 1:1ff.; 1 Sam 10:17–27; 12:1–2ff.). These parallels invariably contributed to Jeremiah's choice to set himself within a prophetic trajectory including Moses and Samuel.[42] Since Jeremiah 1:9 overtly invokes the legislation in Deuteronomy 18:18, there can be no doubt that Jeremiah saw himself as the holder of a prophetic—not priestly—office that Samuel occupied in an earlier time.

While the highly structured form of 1 Samuel 3:21 may be a Deuteronomistic accretion, this is a surface adjustment to a tradition that stands somewhat at odds with other Deuteronomistic texts dealing with prophecy. It is through the divine word (*dabar YHWH*) that these prophets receive and communicate divine will, and it is this same divine word that Samuel's inaugural experience re-establishes among Israel at Shiloh. However, the lexical formula characterizing most of the experience of prophets in the Deuteronomistic History beyond Samuel is *wayyehi dabar YHWH 'el* ("and the word of YHWH came to" so-and-so; e.g., 2 Sam 7:4; 24:11; 1 Kgs 13:20; 17:2, 8; 18:1; 21:17, 28; 2 Kgs 20:4). The only time this formula is applied to Samuel is in a brief Deuteronomistic insertion into 1 Samuel 15:10, part of a chapter that elsewhere shows signs of Deuteronomistic reframing.[43] The formula does not appear at all in 1 Samuel 3. Rather, the author of 1 Samuel 3 informs us that before Samuel was prepared to accept the divine word, it was "not yet revealed to him" (*we-terem yiggaleh 'elayw dabar YHWH*, v. 7), that YHWH was himself revealed to Samuel "through" the divine word (*be-debar YHWH*), and that this was the basis of his renown as a prophet (v. 20).

The *dabar* language in this episode has much in common with the Deuteronomistic *dabar* language as the vehicle for prophetic experience, but it does not fully match it. But this is to be expected if, as argued above, 1 Samuel 1–3 was a pre-Deuteronomistic source. It may have influenced the Deuteronomistic application of the *dabar* language to prophets beyond Shiloh who followed in Samuel's footsteps.[44]

The reliance on Samuel in Jeremiah 15:1 suggests that Jeremianic author perceived a thematic and typological consistency between Samuel and the prophets who followed him in the Deuteronomistic History. Yet it is also clear that Jeremiah drew heavily from the classical prophets, especially those of the 8th century BCE who are not mentioned in the Deuteronomistic History.[45] The Jeremiah tradition thus assumes consistency between Deuteronomistic prophets like Samuel and those whose names were associated with oracles preserved in independent literary troves. However, the differences between these prophets—both in terms of the literary forms attesting to their activity and the non-priestly backgrounds whence most of them came—are difficult to harmonize on a cursory reading. We will therefore explore the putative commonality between Samuel and the collection of the classical prophets from the 8th century on a theme surfacing in all of these sources, namely, the concept and practice of sacrifice.

The classical prophets and Samuel's critique of sacrifice (1 Sam 15:22–3)

One of the most salient features of the narratives regarding Samuel is the prominence of sacrifice. Sacrificial rites stand at the center of every dramatic turn: Elkanah and Hannah come to Shiloh to offer their annual sacrifice (1 Sam 1:3), Eli's sons abuse their authority regarding the meat from sacrificial animals (1 Sam 2:12–16), and Saul encounters Samuel during the course of a local festival and the sacrifice it entails (1 Sam 9:12–24). Saul also crosses the boundary reserved for Samuel regarding the sacrificial devotion before warfare (1 Sam 13:9–10), evoking Samuel's ire and beginning the downward spiral leading to his loss of the right to rule (1 Sam 15). This final episode is especially significant, for at the outset of the chapter, Samuel instructs Saul to engage in a holy war against the Amalekites and to thoroughly eradicate their population:

And Samuel said to Saul: 'YHWH sent me to anoint you to be king over his people, over Israel; now therefore hearken to my words.[46] Thus says YHWH of hosts: I remember that which Amalek did to Israel, how he set himself against him in the way, when he came up out of Egypt. Now go and smite Amalek, and utterly destroy it (*we-haharamto*)[47] ... spare them not, but slay both man and woman, infant and suckling, ox and sheep, camel and ass.' (1 Sam 15:1–2)

The terminology in this passage qualifies the command for warfare as a *herem*, a ritual purge that functions as a form of sacrifice.[48] Battle replaces altar rites, but the end result is the same—an entity (in this case, the Amalekites) is slaughtered as a sign of devotion to YHWH. Though Saul believes that he has carried out this charge faithfully, his subsequent actions meet with Samuel's disapproval, and understandably so, for not only is the Amalekite king Agag taken as a live captive, but Saul's soldiers claim the Amalekite livestock as war spoils (vv. 8–9). Whatever the narrator implies about Saul's expectations and conduct, the end result is that the people under his charge do not live up to the stipulations of Samuel's command.

As a result, Samuel declares that YHWH will rend the monarchy from Saul because the command was not carried out; Samuel then takes the sword and hacks Agag to death, carrying out the divine command himself (v. 33). Samuel's act wrests from Saul the authority to conduct business in the national interest. Yet accompanying this castigation of Saul and the ensuing fallout, we find Samuel offering the following declaration:

> Does YHWH delight in burnt-offerings and sacrifices, as in hearkening to the voice of YHWH? Behold, to obey is better than sacrifice, and to hearken [is better] than the fat of rams. For rebellion is like the sin of witchcraft, and stubbornness is like idolatry and the transgression of [venerating] ancestral icons (*'awon teraphim*). Because you have rejected the word of YHWH, he has also rejected you from being king. (1 Sam 15:22–3)

Though 1 Samuel 15 draws strongly from pre-Deuteronomistic sources,[49] the language in these verses resonates with Deuteronomistic concepts: a ranking of legal obedience over the cult, denigration of idolatry, ancestor veneration (*'awon teraphim*),[50] and unorthodox divination, a focus on the divine word and the expectation that a king should defer to prophetic authority.[51] And of course, placing such a sentiment in the mouth of a prophet like Samuel creates a link to the Deuteronomistic passages where prophets advocate the adherence to YHWH's commandments (2 Kgs 17:13, 23; Jer 7:25; 25:4; 26:5; 35:15).[52]

Nevertheless, we encounter somewhat of a paradox in 1 Samuel 15:22–3. Samuel declares that YHWH is not interested in the sacrifices for which the Amalekite livestock has been captured, yet the entire concept of the *herem* against Amalek is a form of sacrifice, including Samuel's slaying of Agag. Moreover, it is not only the immediate context that is problematized by this statement but the entirety of the Samuel narrative, since we have seen that sacrifice is repeatedly emphasized as an important sacral act. The juxtaposition of an anti-sacrificial declaration in the immediate context of a divine command for a *herem*—and followed in the very next chapter by a scene where Samuel is poised to conduct a sacrifice (1 Sam 16:1–5)—would not have gone unnoticed by an ancient Israelite audience.

The paradox that YHWH demands adherence to his word over sacrifice yet YHWH's word was to *carry out* a form of sacrifice is palpable, especially in light of the preceding and ensuing narratives. A comparison with the words of the 8th-century prophets is helpful in resolving this difficulty. Let us first consider the case of Amos, active ca.755 BCE, whose audiences were the devotees at the royal sanctuary of Bethel. The introductory chapters of Amos suggest deep familiarity with the conventions of the *marzeah*, the ritual feast, in which his audience participates,[53] though these give way to a searing critique of the elite participants and their misguided social predilections. As the book progresses, Amos' oracles become increasingly hostile to the cultic interests of his audience, cresting in his categorical rebuke of their ritual praxes:

> I hate, I despise your feasts, and I will take no delight in your solemn assemblies. Though you offer me burnt offerings and your meal offerings, I will not accept them; neither will I regard the peace offerings of your fat beasts. Take away from me the noise of your songs; and let me not hear the melody of your psalteries. But let justice well up as waters, and righteousness as a mighty stream. Did you bring me sacrifices and offerings in the forty years of the wilderness, O house of Israel? So shall you take up Sikkuth your king and Kaiwan your images, the star of your god, which you made for yourselves. (Amos 5:21–6)

Amos' condemnation of the cult is a rejection of ritual without conviction. In Amos' view, rites and ceremonies conducted at Bethel are devoid of meaning for YHWH because they are not conducted in support of or in conjunction with social ethics and righteousness.[54] Instead, they are reduced to a festishistic act, cult objects to foreign deities (Sakkuth [Sikkuth in the text] and Kaiwan; see further below) fabricated by human hands rather than emanating from the divine.[55] Amos' condemnation of such a disjunction between faith and deed is taken up by Hosea (active ca. 730 BCE), who also prophesied at Bethel and who severely criticized its cultic fixtures:

> O Ephraim, what shall I do to you?... For your goodness is as a morning cloud, and as the dew that quickly passes. Therefore I have hewed them by the prophets, I have slain them by the words of my mouth; and your

judgment goes forth as the light. For I desire devout fidelity, and not sacrifice, and the knowledge of God rather than burnt offerings. But they like men have transgressed the covenant; there have they dealt treacherously against me. (Hos 6:4–7)

Despite the fact that Hosea is a northern Levite while Amos is a Judahite layman, the overlaps in their criticism of the Bethel cult are uncanny. Like Amos, Hosea emphasizes that YHWH's primary concern is adherence to the theological and social dimensions of the covenant rather than ceremonial demonstrations. It is significant, too, that Hosea claims that it is through prophets and their words that YHWH hews down the perpetrators of theological infidelity—in the context of Hosea's larger critique, these are the priests of Bethel, from whom the larger population takes itscues. For Hosea, the cult takes a back seat to heeding the divine *torah*... a *torah* that the priests have failed to impart and that he, as a prophet, now espouses.[56]

The criticism of sacrifice is not limited to prophets active in the north. The Judahite prophets follow suit, addressing different populations in and around Jerusalem in the latter decades of the 8th century BCE, and there are grounds for seeing them influenced by the earlier oracles of Amos and Hosea. As already suggested in chapter 2 of the present study, refugees from the north settled in Judah after the fall of the northern kingdom of Israel, and possibly began doing so in the years leading up to that event.[57] That the oracles of Amos and Hosea have survived in the biblical record is due to their transmission by these refugees,[58] and in light of the destruction of the north these prophetic critiques most certainly commanded the attention of Judahite audiences. Considering the possibility of similar events befalling Judah, both Micah and Isaiah drew from these earlier prophets' words in formulating their own oracles.[59] Micah, especially, sets his message in line with his northern predecessors regarding the viability of sacrifice:

With what shall I come before YHWH, and bow myself before God on high? Shall I come before him with burnt offerings, with year-old calves? Will YHWH be pleased with thousands of rams, with multitudes of rivers of oil? Shall I give my firstborn for my transgression, the fruit of my body for the sin of my soul? It has been told to you, mortal, what YHWH requires of you: only to do justice, to cherish devout fidelity and to walk humbly with your God. (Mic 6:6–8)

Micah's criticism of sacrifice carries an additional dimension not found in the words of his predecessors, namely, the concept of *child* sacrifice. We learn from the Jeremiah tradition that down to the late 7th century BCE, Israelites engaged in child sacrifice or at least viewed it as a viable practice (Jer 7:31–2; 19:4–6, 11–14) and other passages corroborate this as well.[60] Micah's reference to this abhorrent practice, however, serves a powerful rhetorical purpose, for it is set almost casually alongside references to un-objectionable forms of sacrifice. The meta-message is that without following the commandments of YHWH "to do justice, to cherish devout fidelity and to walk humbly," even the seemingly innocuous forms of sacrifice are as abhorrent to YHWH as the slaughter of a child when they are conducted without theological conviction.

Isaiah's condemnation of sacrifice is part of the introductory chapter in the book bearing his name and expressed in an eloquent elegy:

Hear the word of YHWH, you rulers of Sodom; give ear to the law of our God, you people of Gomorrah. To what purpose is the multitude of your sacrifices to me? Says YHWH; I am full of the burnt offerings of rams, and the fat of fed beasts; and I delight not in the blood of bullocks, or of lambs, or of he-goats. When you come to appear before me, who hasrequired this at your hand, to trample my courts? Bring no more vain oblations; it is an offering of abomination to me; new moon and sabbath, the holding of convocations–I cannot endure iniquity along with the solemn assembly. My soul hates your new moons and your appointed seasons; they are a burden to me; I am weary to bear them. And when you spread forth your hands, I will hide my eyes from you; yea, when you make many prayers, I will not hear; your hands are full of blood. Wash yourselves, make yourselves clean, put away the evil of your doings from before my eyes, cease to do evil; Learn to do well; seek justice, relieve the oppressed, judge the fatherless, plead for the widow. (Isa 1:10–17)

Isaiah's oracles generally support the inviolability of Jerusalem, but these words reveal the degree to which the prophet was shaken by empty cultic gestures that distance YHWH from his people. Like Amos, Hosea, and Micah, Isaiah here states that ethical conduct is dear to YHWH, but the beginning of the passage makes no mention of such ethical conduct and indicates that sacrifice had been conducted in its stead, and in such abundance that YHWH had grown sick of such offerings. Isaiah goes on to state that Jerusalem and its population will be redeemed, but these powerful verses attest to his view that ethical conduct, not sacrifice, will bring about this redemption.[61]

In each of these prophetic passages we find a strong xenophobic undercurrent. Amos' likening of empty sacrifice to the formation of cult images of the Mesopotamian deities Sakkuth and Kaiwan introduces a critique of Assyrian religion, and the passage concludes with his warning that Israel will in fact be exiled into Aram, a region that had wrestled to free itself of Assyrian dominance by the mid 8th century BCE with only limited success.[62] Though Micah's mentioning of child sacrifice recalls an Israelite practice,[63] an effort to identify many once-Yahwistic cultic practices as foreign is evident in sources from the late 8th century BCE onward, and Micah's condemnation may factor into this effort.[64] Isaiah, too, begins his criticism by identifying his Israelite audience as the inhabitants of Sodom and Gomorrah, cities that typified "otherness" in opposition to the roots of Israel's ancestry in Genesis 18–19. And though Hosea does not speak explicitly of foreignness in his criticism of sacrifice (Hos 6:6–7), it is set within a larger discourse both within and beyond the chapter that is concerned with Israel's theological infidelity via the influence of foreign religion.[65]

1 Samuel 15 and Israelite ethno-mythology

In the previous chapter of this study, we saw that Levitical tradition preserved a particularly agrarian sense of Israel's ethno-mythology: Israel was "born" through the settling of the highlands, away from the older Canaanite cultures of the lowlands where Egyptian hegemony held sway.[66] In charting the progression of early Israel from their lowland Canaanite roots to their emergence in the highlands, William Dever puts the matter clearly with regard to the prophets of the 8th century BCE and other late monarchic biblical tradents:

> ...the biblical writers enter a vigorous critique, undoubtedly rooted in the pre-Monarchic tradition. Ironically, but not surprisingly, history repeats itself: Monarchic Israel had become precisely the kind of oppressive, elitist state that early Israel came into being to protest, complete with Canaanite style overlords that usurp the land...[67]

Dever makes a crucial further observation:

The Israelite sacrificial system goes back to Canaanite culture...[68]

Dever's comments point to the problem that the prophets of the 8th century BCE addressed in their oracles regarding sacrifice. In each case listed above, the prophet in question sees the rote performance of sacrifice in the official state cult as a regression back to pre-Israelite, foreign status. The aforementioned reference in Judges 21:12 to Shiloh being in "the land of Canaan" indicates how deeply the memory of these foreign social roots remained entrenched in the minds of the biblical authors. As late as the time of Ezekiel in the early 6th century, a reminder of the audience's pre-Israelite foreign ancestry was the height of prophetic rebuke (Ezek 16:3). The invocation of foreign cultures serves as a reminder to the audience of the slippery slope they faced: commitment to the distinctive Israelite agrarian–covenantal ideology is what defined their corporate identity. Without this active commitment, their identity would revert to an undifferentiated, non-Israelite state. A similar sentiment is expressed by the authors of 1 Samuel 12:

And do not turn aside [from YHWH's law (in the context of the larger passage)]; for then you will go after nothingness (*ha-tohu*) which cannot profit nor deliver, for they are nothingness (*tohu*)... But if you shall still do wickedly, both you and your king will be swept away (*tissaphu*). (1 Sam 12:21, 25)

The term *tohu* in this verse is often translated "vain" or "vain things," yet it also carries the semantic meaning "chaos" (see, e.g., Gen 1:2) or, more poignantly, "nothingness."[69] P. Kyle McCarter sees this as a fairly late addition to the text, since this same term is found in late texts such as Isaiah 41:29 that critique foreign idol worship.[70] However, *tohu* is entirely appropriate in an earlier context for 1 Samuel 12, as the term identifies the maintenance of YHWH's covenant law as the basis for national existence. Without this, the institution of the monarchy may lead to a reversion to pre-Israelite conditions predating the flight to the highlands... that is, no Israel at all.[71]

David Tsumura has stated that the term *tohu* in 1 Samuel 12:21 "has nothing to do with the concept of 'chaos' as the counterpart to 'order'," arguing exclusively for reading *tohu* as "nothingness."[72] Yet the two readings are not at odds with each other. Exodus 15 conceives of Israel's eisodus into the highlands and consequent corporate existence as a sort of mythic creation in its own right, with the Egypto-Canaanite threats relegated to the waters of chaos.[73] 1 Samuel 12:25 appears to allude to this very idea via the double entendre *tissaphu*, "you will be swept away," echoing the *yam suph* of Exodus 15:4, the mythic waters of chaos that sweep away the foreign threat to Israel's existence.

Tohu may therefore serve double-duty, representing *both* "chaos" and "nothingness" with respect to what Israel will become by ignoring the forces that propelled them into the highlands. Samuel reminds his audience that they, like him, hold a liminal position: it is the ideas that he communicates which hold them in the balance between life in the land and dissolution into nothingness. This appears to come close to the same critique that the 8th-century prophets lodge at the cultic practices promoted by state cults of their own day. In both cases, it is the pitfalls of monarchy and its emulation of foreign social values that compromise the covenant with YHWH and Israel's ethno-mythology.

All of this informs how we must read the redactor's inclusion of vv. 22–3 of sacrifice into 1 Samuel 15. As Schloen notes, a close connection existed between Amalekites and Israelites in the pre-state period that eventually dissolved into hostility with the solidification of Israel's monarchic institutions.[74] Texts such as Exodus 17:8–16 and Deuteronomy 25:17–19 must be viewed in light of the memory of this schism: despite notable differences, both agree that Israelite religious and social identity is contingent upon the full separation of Israel from Amalek.[75] Saul's failure to carry out the *herem* against Amalek thus symbolizes his inability to maintain Israelite ethnic integrity even—or perhaps especially—with the new mechanism of the monarchy available to him. By contrast, Samuel's initial oracle containing the *herem* command and his subsequent slaying of Agag (1 Sam 15:33) demonstrates his own commitment to maintaining those boundaries and, by consequence, Israel's otherwise tenuous existence.

Saul's capture of Agag is important in this schematizing of the episode. Saul's behavior is expected in relation to ancient near eastern military conduct, where kings were captured before being executed or imprisoned.[76] From Saul's purview, this was part and parcel of the *herem*-act, but in conforming to standard foreign praxis, the very purpose of the *herem* is compromised, and ethnic boundaries are blurred. Saul's choice to follow conventional warfare conduct quite literally makes him "a king like all the nations," the type that Samuel warned would ultimately separate Israel from its unique relationship with YHWH (1 Sam 8:18).[77] With the addition of 1 Samuel 15:22–3, Samuel's prophetic warning several chapters earlier already begins to see its fulfillment. From the Deuteronomistic perspective, 1 Samuel 15 *in toto* ratifies Samuel's position as a true Mosaic prophet (Deut 18:19–22), and the Levite–priestly perspective voiced in Samuel's earlier rebuke of kingship is rendered an authentic prophecy.

Finally, as already discussed, the Deuteronomists envisioned a society where prophets stood at the top of the political hierarchy.[78] It is thus fitting for Samuel to take a symbolic stand in this narrative for prophets as the true leaders of the nation by completing the *herem*-act himself. In so doing, the narrative credits the integrity of the Israelite state not to kings, but to prophets—an idea echoed later in the redaction of the book of Kings as well (2 Kgs 17:13, 23; 21:10; 24:2). For the Deuteronomistic redactors, Samuel's oracle, critique, and act were consistent with the rhetoric of the 8th-century prophets who similarly took monarchic culture to task for adopting postures reminiscent of foreign nations. The interpolation of 1 Samuel 15:22–3 into the narrative turns Samuel into a predecessor for these later prophets, identifying monarchy as an institution that must be subordinate to covenantal standards preserved by YHWH's prophetic servants. Taking this one step further, and considering Samuel's completion of the *herem*-act (v. 33) and Monroe's observation that the *herem* was associated with state formation, the episode implies that Samuel is the true leader of the monarchy, even if he is not a monarch—a concept reminiscent of Deuteronomy 17:18–20.[79]

In sum

There is much connecting the depiction of Samuel's prophetic characteristics to his status as a Levite. Both prophets and Levites act as intercessors between Israel and YHWH, teaching the people divine *torah* and praying on their behalf to the deity in times of need. But the rise of the monarchy was a game-changing event that saw the prophecy surface in distinction from the priesthood that eventually fell under royal command. As with the role reserved for Levites in the pre-monarchic period, it became the role of the prophet to serve as a sentinel over the nation and alert it when it was in danger of losing touch with the values that had always defined it.[80]

Samuel's experiences as a Levite priest were re-imagined as a paradigm of prophecy by the Deuteronomists. It is for this reason that when later writers such as Jeremiah and Ezekiel direct their ire at the folly of the late pre-exilic kings, they do so as prophets rather than as priests. By their day, the critique of kings and of unorthodox religious behavior had been normalized into the prophetic category initiated, at least in the historiographic sources, by Samuel. The authority to critique kings, to interpret law, and to convey new directives from YHWH invariably provided the prophet with the power to sit as a judge on behalf of YHWH as well. It is to this aspect of Samuel's legacy that we now turn our attention.

4

Samuel as a Judge

Guide the future by the past,
Long ago the mould was cast.

—Rush "Bastille Day"

As noted previously, the Deuteronomistic History presents the first several chapters of the book of Samuel as a continuation of the book of Judges:[1] Samuel's actions in 1 Samuel 7:3–4 finally put an end to the cycle of decline that is introduced in Judges 2:11–19.[2] There can be little doubt, too, that the redactor of the first few chapters of the book of Samuel shaped his sources with an eye to the Judges narrative more generally, since the depiction of Eli at his death specifies that he "judged Israel for forty years" (1 Sam 4:18). This formula is similar to those summarizing the activity of the major figures in the book of Judges, but it is essential to define what we mean by the term "judge" (Hebrew *šophet*), as it carries a multiplicity of meanings in different textual contexts. In loose terms, a *šophet* in ancient Israel could be a member of the judiciary, a royal figure, a priest, a clan elder, a sage, and probably other social types.[3] In what follows, we will consider a few aspects of what is implied with the term *šophet*, and how it functions as a catch-all of sorts that, from the Deuteronomistic point of view, brought together different streams of tradition through its application to Samuel.

Biblical law and Israelite jurisprudence

The root for the term *šophet* is *špt*, regularly associated with law and jurisprudence in biblical literature, and which lies at the etymological heart of the term *mišpat*—"legal ruling" or "custom" in a variety of passages. There is no shortage of witnesses to the juridical role of both prophets and Levites in the Hebrew Bible in relation to the declaration of rulings/*mišpatim*. Samuel himself refers to the divine decree regarding the shift to monarchy as the *mišpat hamelekh*, "the rule regarding the king" (1 Sam 8:11), and later writes down the legal terms of the monarchy, the *mišpat hamelukha* (1 Sam 10:25). Deuteronomy 33:8–11, a passage we have already considered in relation to the Levites, carries a decidedly juridical character:

> Thy *thummim* and thy *'urim* be with thy holy one...
> They shall teach Jacob thine ordinances (*mišpatekha*), and Israel thy law...
> They shall put incense before thee, and whole burnt-offering upon thine altar.... (Deut 33:8, 10)

The Levite here is given charge over three aspects of juridical processes—divination (the *thummim* and *'urim*, or ritual lots), legal authority, and executive agency. Scholars therefore often view Levites as holding important judicial roles along with the other social types enumerated above. As discussed in the chapter on Samuel as a Levite, their juridical authority was rooted in the saintly numinous status they claimed as representatives of the divine. Samuel's background as a Levite carries with it the aforementioned juridical duties, but the biblical record also associates judicial status with the *production* of law through figures empowered by the divine; in most ancient cultures, this was a royal prerogative.[4] The royal production of law was meant to cultivate a type of civic or sacral mentality associated with the royal lawgiver as a representative of the divine order. The law may be described as top–down in its depiction of the monarch/subject social dynamic, that is, law emanates from the king down to the commoner for the latter to revere as a symbol of the king's divinely mandated status.[5]

While biblical law is very much indebted to ancient near eastern legal trends, it breaks significantly with older precedent in this regard: though there is certainly a theoretical dimension to the laws in the

Pentateuch, the laws are presented as the expression of a covenant between YHWH and Israel with the pragmatic purpose of maintaining Israel's tenure on their land, not to cultivate concepts of the royal hierarchy. Furthermore, while much of the legislation in Exodus–Numbers evidences a top–down dynamic (YHWH declares the law, Moses delivers it, and the people must do it), some cases witness the legal process as a more populist institution. Let us consider, for example, the case of the blasphemer in the Leviticus 24:

> And the son of an Israelite woman, whose father was an Egyptian, went out among the children of Israel; and the son of the Israelite woman and an Israelite man strove together in the camp. And the son of the Israelite woman blasphemed the [divine] name, and cursed; and they brought him to Moses... and they put him in ward, that it [the verdict] might be declared to them at the mouth of YHWH. And YHWH spoke to Moses, saying: 'Bring forth him that hath cursed without the camp; and let all that heard him lay their hands upon his head, and let all the congregation stone him. And you shall speak to the children of Israel, saying: Whosoever curses his God shall bear his sin... You shall have one manner of law, for the stranger as for the native; for I am YHWH your God.' And Moses spoke to the children of Israel, and they brought forth from the camp him that had cursed, and stoned him with stones. And the children of Israel did as YHWH commanded Moses. (Lev 24:10–23)

In this brief narrative, the community is unsure of how to punish an individual of mixed ethnicity who engages in a blasphemous act. The community then approaches Moses to determine what to do, and Moses in turn obtains a new law from YHWH to address the matter. Once Moses conveys the divine command, the people carry out the verdict. In this episode, Moses is certainly a judge insofar as he articulates to Israel the divine ruling on the matter, but he does so by virtue of communal prompting and need. Though there are textual witnesses to Israel's kings laying claim to juridical rights that are consistent with general ancient near eastern trends, the above-mentioned Leviticus passage preserves a tradition where law derives from the needs of the public, and similar cases can be found in other Pentateuchal passages.[6]

Even though the Leviticus passage above emanates from a Priestly author, it has much in common with the attitude toward monarchy in the prophetic literature and the Deuteronomistic History. Like those traditions, it carries forward the echo of Israel's early ideology that formed in contradistinction to Late Bronze Age kingship, and removes law and jurisprudence from the social strata associated with royalty. In this passage, there is nary a mention of the tent-shrine of the wilderness otherwise prominent as a locus of jurisprudence in Leviticus; law is produced well beyond any indication of a sanctuary that could be viewed as symbolic of a royal temple or court (compare to Amos 7:13). Furthermore, justice is served when the community and YHWH function in dialogue with each other via the right ombudsman. The juridical agent—Moses in the case of Leviticus 24—is the ombudsman between the two.[7]

This same concept is found in Deuteronomy. In Deuteronomy 16:18–20, local sacral agents function as the bearers of Moses' authority in applying the law among the lay public. Though a trip to the central sanctuary may secure new rulings (Deut 17:8–13),[8] Deuteronomy does not conceive of this sanctuary as a royally sponsored temple, the procuring of new law is entirely initiated in the popular sphere, and it is within the popular sphere that its enactment will purge the land of evil (Deut 17:12). We thus encounter in biblical law vestiges of an egalitarian concept of jurisprudence situated well beyond the precincts of the monarchy, identified with public prompting and prophetic responses. This dovetails with the tradition of Samuel as a Levite and as a prophet. 1 Samuel 7:15–17 identifies him as a circuit-court jurist, Samuel's speech in 1 Samuel 12 overtly ties his ideological predilections to the legal theology of Deuteronomy (vv. 20bβ, 24–5), and some measure of law-giving is credited to him with the document in 1 Samuel 10:25. It seems natural, then, that the Deuteronomists identified him as the last of the judges, suggesting that his type of leadership represented the ideal form of pre-monarchic governance; as adduced in the previous chapter, the Deuteronomists thereby position Samuel as a "new" Moses, significantly re-shaping the old Moses–Samuel parallel in 1 Samuel 1–3, but preserving its implications for Israelite legal thought.

Deconstructing the depiction of Samuel as a judge

The aforementioned Deuteronomistic tableau, however, is no accurate account of the past. We must bear in mind that the biblical legal

Samuel as a Judge 67

idiom in which the Deuteronomists operate is a product of the late 8th through mid 6th centuries BCE, long after the time of Samuel's alleged activity and a good deal of time after many of the narratives about him were composed.[9] The Pentateuchal texts mentioned above cannot be used to reconstruct how a figure like Samuel, in his own day, would have "judged" Israel. The problem is amplified when we look to Samuel's ostensible peers, the major warrior–saviors in the book of Judges. Few of the narratives in the book of Judges reveal any legal interest or activity on the part of the major characters (the exception being Deborah in Judg 4:4–5, on which see below). The typology of "judge" in the book of Judges does not come into contact with what would become the dominant understanding of jurisprudence as depicted in the biblical law of later periods.

The problem expands when we look more closely at how the language of "judging" is applied to Samuel. 1 Samuel 8 connects the *špt* terminology to jurisprudence via the critique of Samuel's sons (vv. 1–4), but the language of these verses is highly Deuteronomistic (compare to Deut 16:18–20), and the ensuing verse, wherein the people request a king, is similarly indebted to the language of Deuteronomy (compare 1 Sam 8:5 to Deut 17:15–16).[10] Nevertheless, the pre-Deuteronomistic tradition later in 1 Samuel 8 relates the *špt* language to royal military leadership (v. 19), and the account of Samuel's successful leadership in the previous chapter exhibits a similar conceptual gulf (1 Sam 7). The 1 Samuel 7 passage demands special attention. Following a brief Deuteronomistic introduction we encounter the account of a battle against the Philistines:

And they gathered together to Mizpah, and drew water, and poured it out before YHWH, and fasted on that day, and said there: 'We have sinned against YHWH.' And Samuel judged *(wayyišpot)* the children of Israel in Mizpah...And Samuel took a sucking lamb, and offered it for a whole burnt-offering unto YHWH; and Samuel cried unto YHWH for Israel; and YHWH answered him. And as Samuel was offering up the burnt-offering, the Philistines drew near to battle against Israel; but YHWH thundered with a great thunder on that day upon the Philistines, and discomfited them; and they were smitten down before Israel...So the Philistines were subdued, and they came no more within the border of Israel; and the hand of YHWH was against the Philistines all the days of Samuel. (1 Sam 7:5–13)

There is nothing in this passage that speaks to the juridical process. Rather, the phrase *wayyišpot* pertains to Samuel's ritual appeal to YHWH, who routes out the enemy.[11] As in 1 Samuel 8:19, "judging" here is connected to warfare; in this case, Samuel's "judging" invokes the presence of the divine warrior. This takes us closer to the function of the term in the book of Judges as opposed to the Pentateuchal passages discussed above. If Israel's requested king is also to be a warrior, then a literary link is formed between king and warrior–savior via the sociological typology termed "chieftain." These sociopolitical leaders sat at the top of extended local lineages and governed in geographically limited areas through military prowess and claims to sacral authority.[12] It was chieftains who held power in the days before the shift to kingship, and some scholars believe that the earliest kings were themselves chieftains who managed to extend their power beyond the strictures of chiefdoms.[13]

Many of the major figures in the book of Judges appear to conform to this typology: their life-long governance (Judg 2:18) is secured through success in battle, and in at least one case (that of Gideon) this leads to sacralization, i.e., the prerogative to officiate as a representative of and to the divine (Judg 8:23–32). Moreover, and despite the text claiming their judging "Israel" or "all Israel," the judges' geographical jurisdiction was limited.[14] Yet while Samuel is clearly a sacral figure and exercises authority over extended kinship networks in a relatively limited area (the Ephraimite/northern Benjaminite territory in 1 Sam 7:16–17), he is not a chieftain who stands at the head of these groups. Like Eli before him, he is set aside from the kinship groups over whom chieftains held sway and mediates between them.

By "fronting" the narrative in 1 Samuel 7 with language that points back to the book of Judges (1 Sam 7:3–4), the Deuteronomistic redactors have created the impression that Samuel was the last of the warrior–saviors depicted in the book of Judges.[15] Moreover, Samuel's valedictory address in 1 Samuel 12 does much to solidify his position within the pantheon of these warrior–saviors, identifying him with this earlier form of leadership (v. 11).[16] The redactor has highlighted the commonalities that Samuel shares with several of the major figures in the book of Judges—pre-monarchic temporality, association with battle, priestly or prophetic qualities. But one must pause before accepting these as genuinely common features facilitating Samuel's inclusion, for in addition to the differences noted above, other important differences are found lurking beneath the surface of the text.

Let us first consider the matter of sacral status and cultic authority. Samuel's role as a priest is never cast in a negative light, but is highlighted throughout the narratives. We first encounter him as an infant left in Eli's charge and as the narrative moves forward, the narrator reports that his cultic stature grows in step: he obtains priestly vestments (1 Sam 2:11), takes on the responsibility of night watch over the Ark of YHWH (1 Sam 3), and of course eventually serves as the conduit to YHWH via his oracular skill (1 Sam 3:21; 4:1). This leads, finally, to his role as priestly intercessor, praying and sacrificing on behalf of the nation to YHWH with abundant success (1 Sam 7:2–13), which leads to the affirmation of his status as a judge in the narrative (1 Sam 7:15). However, all of these elements stand *against* the depiction of cultic behavior among the major figures in the book of Judges, especially two who receive overt mention in 1 Samuel 12:11, Gideon (Jerubbaal in the text) and Jephtah. Gideon's success on the battlefield leads him to assume position as chieftain, which he consecrates through his cultic initiatives:[17]

And Gideon made an *ephod*... and put it in his city, in Ophrah; and all Israel whored after it there; and it became a snare to Gideon, and to his house. (Judg 8:27)

The redactor pulls no punches in describing the deleterious effects of this cultic installation, i.e., that it contributes to Israel's path down the road to ruin. The language used to describe the effect of Gideon's cult site—that Israel "whored" after it and that it became a "snare" to Gideon and his kinship network—is precisely the language Hosea later uses to castigate the corrupt northern state cult and its personnel in his 8th–century BCE oracles (Hos 9:8).[18] The cultic activity revolves around an item called an *ephod*, the same term applied to the priestly vestment for which Samuel receives a supportive nod from the narrator.[19] But whereas Samuel's *ephod* contributes to his sacral legitimacy, Gideon's is cast in the worst possible light, identifying Gideon's assumption of cultic responsibility as a dangerous affair.

Jephtah, too, spells trouble from the moment he appears: he is a social outcast (Judg 11:1) whose thuggish resources are levied against the needs of his father's clan for security from foreign threats.[20] While this may well relate to the measures a chieftain had to undertake in order to establish his dominion, it does little to leave the impression that Jephtah's new social station brings him legitimate sacral status. The act of warfare conducted by Jephtah is done for personal gain rather than in the interests of the people or in the name of YHWH; the brutality of his cultic act—human sacrifice—is a narrative expression of this degeneracy. That the victim is his own daughter is an ironic twist, which suggests that his goals as deliverer have little to do with securing conditions for Israel's fruitful existence, a major concern in virtually every dimension of the Israelite cult.[21] In the cases of both Jephtah and Gideon, the judges' cultic endeavors serve as the low-point in the execution of their office, in polar opposition to Samuel's public turn as a "judge" in 1 Samuel 7.

Even more poignant is the role of prophecy in the book of Judges. We have seen that it is ultimately as a prophet that Samuel is best remembered within the Deuteronomistic tradition, which draws from his prophetic prominence in the pre-Deuteronomistic sources. By contrast, there is a surprising paucity of prophets in the book of Judges. The book mentions only two prophets—Deborah (Judg 4–5) and an anonymous prophet who appears at the beginning of Judges 6. The words spoken by this prophet warrant attention:

And it came to pass, when the children of Israel cried to YHWH because of Midian, that YHWH sent a prophet (*'iš nabi'*) to the children of Israel; and he said to them: 'Thus says YHWH, the God of Israel: I brought you up from Egypt, and brought you forth out of the house of bondage; and I delivered you out of the hand of the Egyptians, and out of the hand of all that oppressed you, and drove them out from before you, and gave you their land. And I said to you: I am YHWH your God; you shall not fear the gods of the Amorites, in whose land you dwell; but you have not hearkened to my voice.' (Judg 6:8–10)

This prophetic speech is clear Deuteronomistic prose, highlighting the Exodus and the tradition of conquest as the basis for Israel's piety and allegiance to YHWH. The speech concludes with "but you have not hearkened to my voice," very much in keeping with the

Deuteronomistic introduction to the book of Judges in Judges 2:11–19. The appearance of this anonymous prophet continues the idea of prophetic leadership from the Deborah tradition in the previous two chapters, since Deborah would otherwise be the sole prophet to receive mention in the book of Judges. Yet unlike Deborah, who is a major character in the two chapters dealing with the events of her day, this prophet is never heard from again, and the words of his speech seem generic rather than pertinent to the specifics of the Gideon narrative that follows.

Since prophecy and monarchy were intimately intertwined, the appearance of this prophet may have been included into this episode because of the quasi-monarchic dimensions of the Gideon tradition. The closing verses of Judges 8 hint rather strongly that Gideon attempted to establish a chiefdom with royal potential, and as we have seen, the name of his son in Judges 9, Abimelekh ("my father [is] king") seems to confirm this.[22] The Gideon–Abimelekh chiefdom is remembered as a failed attempt at establishing kingship; the introduction of the anonymous prophet at the beginning of the narrative looks ahead to this attempt and provides an interpretive framework for seeing it as a socio-religious relapse. In a way, this anticipates Samuel's rebuke of kingship in 1 Samuel 8 before Saul's rise to power, but unlike the Samuel–Saul dynamic, the anonymous prophet in question is not part of the ensuing action, and there is nothing to indicate that Gideon even knew of a prophet active in his day. Moreover, unlike Samuel, the anonymous prophet is not the central savior in the narrative. That role belongs to Gideon, who is never identified in prophetic terms.

All of this suggests that the anonymous prophet is simply a Deuteronomistic literary device.[23] It thus seems that only Deborah is a prophet–judge like Samuel, but even this requires scrutiny. The ancient tradition in Judges 5 may lead to the conclusion that Deborah was regarded as a sacral figure,[24] and the fact that the poem is attributed to her in the canonical form of the book of Judges implies that she was among the prophetic personalities to whom the singing of sacred verse is attributed.[25] This, however, is a late feature of biblical consciousness, since the poem in Judges 5 was only placed in Deborah's mouth when redacted into its Deuteronomistic context. The connection between the poem in Judges 5 and Deborah may not have been a *de facto* prophetic qualification, especially if, as some have argued, Deborah's name was introduced into the poem at a secondary stage in its development.[26]

What, then, of the notice in Judges 4 where Deborah is overtly identified as a "prophetess"? The verses in question, which introduce her into the tale, leave no doubt as to her prophetic status within the narrative:

> Now Deborah, a prophetess, the wife of Lappidoth, she judged Israel at that time. And she sat under the palm-tree of Deborah between Ramah and Bethel in the hill country of Ephraim; and the children of Israel came up to her for judgment. (Judg 4:4–5)

This passage can be read at face value regarding Deborah as a "prophetess." It is certainly the case that Barak will only go into battle if Deborah, as YHWH's representative, accompanies him, and Deborah makes the prediction that credit for the victory over the enemies will be given to a woman (Yael the Kenite, as we will later learn), not to him.[27] However, the language of Judges 4:4–5 is virtually identical to the introduction of Huldah, the prophet consulted by King Josiah's agents in 2 Kings 22, a Deuteronomistic narrative:[28]

> Now Deborah, *a prophetess ('išah nebi'ah), the wife of* Lappidoth, she judged Israel at that time. *And she dwelt* under the palm-tree of Deborah.... (Judg 4:4–5)

> So Hilkiah the priest...went unto Huldah, *a prophetess ('išah nebi'ah), the wife of* Shallum...*and she dwelt* in Jerusalem in the second quarter.... (2 Kgs 22:14)

It is striking that the author of 2 Kings 22 uses the same lexical formula to describe Huldah as that used to describe Deborah. If the same scribe or group of scribes is responsible for both passages, then the explicit depiction of Deborah as a "prophetess" (*'išah nebi'ah*) may be a rhetorical attempt to provide Huldah with a venerable forerunner, thereby projecting late standards into an early tradition.[29] This does not mean that the early Deborah tradition did not remember her as bearing oracular or divinatory ability.[30] But the overt identification of her as an *'išah nebi'ah* alongside the same terms applied to Huldah strongly suggests that the *'išah nebi'ah* moniker stems from a redactional hand.[31]

If the term *'išah nebi'ah* is a redactional accretion, what sort of religious office (replete with oracular, juridical authority) did Deborah hold in the pre-Deuteronomistic tradition? As some commentators on the book of Judges have noted, a feature in Deborah's identification—that she is the "wife of Lappidoth"—could carry an earlier meaning deliberately obscured by the scribe. The Hebrew word *lappidoth* means "flames," and some suggest that the phrase originally was understood as "Deborah, a fiery woman," i.e., a commanding figure with a fiery personality.[32] Yet mythological lore in Israelite religion often associates YHWH's warrior characteristics with fire, lightning, and other combustive phenomena (Hab 3:5; Ps 29; Exod 19:16–19; Deut 5:4–5), and the ancient tradition in Judges 5 plays upon this mythological lore in its depiction of the battle involving Deborah and Barak as well (Judg 5:15).[33]

This mythic dimension survives in the narrative notice of Judges 4:4: the association of Deborah with *lappidoth* may have initially connected her character to the mythological realm as a numinous figure with oracular power. In this case, just as the Deuteronomistic redactors repackaged Samuel's Levitical role as primarily prophetic in nature, they have done the same here with Deborah, casting her in a manner identical to Huldah (replete with a named "husband"). As with the shaping of the Samuel tradition, this is a late literary flourish, an attempt to galvanize disparate sacral legacies into a united prophetic front for the benefit of a readership at temporal distance to the events depicted in the narratives.[34]

We also encounter discrepancies between Samuel and the other judges with a feature often identified with the type of leadership represented in the book of Judges, namely, that of the "charismatic" sort. Charismatic leadership was defined long ago by the sociologist Max Weber as a group identification of supernatural or extraordinary abilities with an individual under whose guidance the group is mobilized and directed.[35] In the book of Judges, such leadership is indicated by the common lexical formula "the divine spirit (*ruah 'elohim*) was upon" so-and-so, identifying the warrior–savior in question as somehow under the direct inspiration or guidance of YHWH.[36] This charismatic state is often identified with prophetic modalities of ecstatic behavior, but it seems to manifest in the traditions in the book of Judges as the basis for military leadership and, eventually, claims to chieftainship.

It is therefore important to note that Samuel is never depicted in this manner.[37] The episode involving his inaugural encounter with YHWH is not presented as an entrance into an altered state of consciousness. As discussed in the previous chapter, Samuel's prophetic experience is characterized by the divine word (*dabar YHWH*), not the divine spirit (*ruah 'elohim*). Subsequent episodes involving Samuel's prophetic capabilities reinforce this distinction: whenever Samuel offers a prophetic pronouncement, it is in the form of a clear directive or measured (if periodically angry) response (1 Sam 8; 12; 13:13–14; 15:10, 22–3). Even when Samuel appears alongside ecstatic prophets, he is not described as participating in their ecstasy, but as serving as their overseer (1 Sam 19:20).[38] Indeed, it is Saul, not Samuel, who is possessed by the divine spirit when he encounters the ecstatic cult prophets (1 Sam 10:10–12) and before his raising of the tribal muster (1 Sam 11:6)—an important point to which we will return below.

We also should recall the words of Hosea in the 8th century BCE, who draws categorical distinctions between the ecstatic prophets ("then man of the spirit is mad") and the prophet as a sentinel (*zopheh ephraim*) in Hosea 9:7–8.[39] Samuel's lineage roots identify him as one such *zopheh* (*ben zuph* in 1 Sam 1:1) and he maintains these affiliations later in life as well (Saul finds him living in *'eretz zuph*, "the land of Zuph," in 1 Sam 9:4–5). Though *zuph* in these texts may be the name of a kinship group, this does not preclude the possibility of cultic function as a constitutive element of kinship construction.[40] Such is, as we have seen, what lies beneath the assimilation of outside individuals into priestly clans or the merging of one priestly genealogy into that of another. In addition, the biblical record often identifies specific sacral praxes and traditions with particular kinship groups; one thinks of the Rechabites' tent-dwelling in 2 Kings 9 or the notice regarding the scribal clans in 1 Chronicles 2:55. The old prophetic legends in Kings also seem to conceive of the prophets in terms of kinship.[41]

All of this accounts for the etymological connection between Hosea's *zopheh* in Hosea 9:8 and *ben zuph/'eretz zuph* in 1 Samuel 1:1/9:5, respectively. If the *zopheh* of Hosea is an established prophetic category defined in contradistinction to the ecstatic prophets, then this may be related to the narrative depiction of Samuel, a *ben zuph*, in a similar manner. The depiction of Samuel as a political leader standing in intimate proximity to the supernatural may fall under Weber's classification of "charismatic" in terms of public recognition of his supernatural qualities, but not because the divine spirit moved him into an altered state of consciousness, at least as far as the text is concerned.

Finally, the question of military engagement as a hallmark of "judgeship" requires attention. In every major episode of the book of Judges, the judge in question leads the Israelite forces into battle or is, like Samson, a formidable vehicle of physical force. It is certainly the case that Samuel's leadership position connected to national military confrontations is a central tenet of his authority (1 Samuel 7), and provides a contrast to the ineffectual role played by the Elides under whose watch the Ark was earlier captured in battle (1 Samuel 4). However, it is YHWH who actually leads the charge (through a thundering that scatters the enemy). Samuel does not step onto the battlefield the same way that Ehud, Deborah and Barak, Gideon, Jephtah, or even Samson do.[42] He secures divine sponsorship through prayer and sacrifice (1 Sam 7:5–13), but the only time Samuel is presented as engaging in bloodshed is with the killing of Agag, after the battle with the Amalekites is over (1 Sam 15:33). His inclusion into the ranks of the judges cannot therefore be attributed to his legacy as a warrior, despite his cultic association with battle.

Levites vs. chieftains as judges

It is clear from the foregoing examples that Samuel's place as a judge in the Deuteronomistic presentation of the pre-monarchic period draws from cosmetic similarities between him and the warrior–saviors in the book of Judges. We must ask, therefore, why the redactors involved in this process went to such lengths to shape both narratives of the book of Judges and the Samuel narratives as contiguous if the differences between Samuel and his predecessors are so varied and considerable. The answer is to be found not in Samuel's connection to the figures that precede him, but to the one that succeeded him as the nation's political leader: Saul. The literary expression of the relationship between both characters addresses a larger issue regarding the balance of power in the shift to monarchy, and one that remained on the minds of the later redactors who compiled the literary traditions concerning both figures.

The narratives depicting the tensions between Samuel and Saul may be seen as a window into the competing forms of leadership vested in the offices of Levite and chieftain. Saul's rise to power is described in the book of Samuel as a matter of divine designation through prophetic agency in 1 Samuel 9:1–10:16, but the earliest account of his rise to prominence in 1 Samuel 11 more closely matches the chieftain model. Saul is presented in terms very similar to the warrior–saviors of the book of Judges:[43] a foreign oppressor rises over the community, the divine spirit descends upon him, and his amalgamation of the Israelite militia and his battlefield success points to charismatic-type leadership.[44] Though the narrative in 1 Samuel 11 was likely composed with awareness of the traditions regarding other warrior–saviors attested in the book of Judges,[45] it speaks to the stages of accomplishment that Saul was required to pass in order to eventually command allegiance and recognition as a political leader imbued with divinely derived power.

All of these factors combine to present Saul as a *nagid*, a warrior–king-elect,[46] a role that expands upon that of a chieftain. 1 Samuel 11 links Saul to the chieftains of the book of Judges, but there are indications that Saul already came from a family that held an exalted chieftainship before he rose to broader prominence. 1 Samuel 9:1 twice emphasizes that Saul's lineage is Benjaminite. Bodner comments that within the Deuteronomistic History, this could be a potential slant against him,[47] and it is indeed the case that biblical tradition often identifies Benjaminite status as grounds for humility. On the pre-Deuteronomistic level, however, the very opposite may have been the case. The Benjaminites in earliest Israel are probably the genealogical and cultural descendants of the Yaminites of Mari, a Bronze Age monarchic culture that had established residence in the Canaanite highlands centuries earlier.[48] Claims to Benjaminite status in pre-monarchic Israel would therefore have carried a prestige that accompanied firmly established social traditions and longstanding lineage roots, and this is affirmed by the lengthy genealogical details provided for Saul's family in 1 Samuel 9:1.[49] Furthermore, 1 Samuel 9:1

reveals that Saul's father Kish is a *gibbor hayil*, a "mighty man of valor," an honorific title used to describe the status of the wealthy and powerful in Israelite society and which indicates chieftain status as well.[50]

Saul's residence at Gibeah is also indicative of his function as a chieftain. Though 1 Samuel 13–14 present him as facing off against the Philistines, the Philistines probably had initially employed Saul as a local chieftain capable of providing them with access to Benjaminite territory during their period of domination.[51] As Siegfried Kreutzer has argued, the location of Gibeah at the fringe of Benjaminite territory but close to Philistine territory places Saul in geographic proximity to the dominant Philistine power, indicating that he possessed resources that they could exploit before he eventually turned against them.[52] These pieces of evidence point to the likelihood that Kish had been a Benjaminite chieftain who passed his status on to Saul. His success against the Ammonites in 1 Samuel 11 literarily reaffirms his chieftainship and justifies the measures he took to parlay it into the basis for a fledgling monarchic proto-state.[53]

The literary parallels between Samuel and Saul (e.g., 1 Sam 1:1; 9:1) are often recognized by scholars as a redactor's attempt to anticipate Saul's rise to power in the account of Samuel's own origin narrative.[54] But the parallels also suggest competition between the forms of leadership represented by each character.[55] Both Levites and chieftains received deference from local lineages groups, both commanded juridical authority, and both carried sacral responsibilities (one through successful holy war, the other through numinous-saintly recognition). But beyond the competition these similarities imply, the greatest source of tension would have rested on ideological/theological grounds. We have seen that the Levites originated as an institution to safeguard Israelite social interests against hierarchies that could lead to the abuse of sacral power. This, in turn, was a reaction against the Late Bronze Age Egypto-Canaanite monarchies where such abuses and their effects were remembered in early Israel.

By contrast, the office of chieftain carried much closer ties to Egypto-Canaanite social structures. Robert Miller has discussed that the early Israelite chiefdoms were secondary derivatives of the power structures held by Canaanite regents of Egypt in the Late Bronze Age.[56] Though Egypt's imperial control diminished significantly at the outset of the Iron Age, it never fully disappeared, and as Richard E. Friedman wrote many years ago, the entire history of Israel as envisioned by the Deuteronomists was essentially framed by the ongoing presence of Egypt looming in the background.[57] The Song of Deborah suggests as much with its wordplay on the term "Pharaoh" in the opening line of Judges 5:2 (*biphro'ah pera'oth be-yisra'el*).[58] For the poet, Egyptian imperial echoes remained in Israelite consciousness, and those who descended from families once empowered by the Egypto-Canaanite administrative system would certainly have held a degree of social influence even in the transitional period of the early Iron Age. As such, chieftains in early Israel may have settled away from lowland Canaanite cities, but the foundation of their power was rooted in earlier positions of influence they carried with them in the flight to the highland frontier.

With this background in mind, it is understandable why the different biblical authors behind the Saul and Samuel traditions either highlight the conflict between them or apologetically attempt to diminish it: in more ways than one, the forms of leadership characterizing Samuel and Saul represented mutually exclusive social visions. This conflict is itself implied within the first few verses of the narrative's introduction of Saul. The well-known wordplay invoking the terms *nagid* and *nabi'* within 1 Samuel 9 is not simply a matter of literary punning or the foreshadowing of later events in Saul's life, but is suggestive of the countenancing of the leadership typologies represented by the narrative's *nagid* (Saul) and its *nabi'* (Samuel).[59] By later reporting Saul's own prophetic encounter and experience (1 Sam 10:10–12) the narrator makes a case for Saul's hierarchical hegemony over the prophets and, by extension, the cultic fixtures of the area hitherto under the control of Samuel.

The larger Deuteronomistic shaping of the book of Samuel makes similar suggestions. 1 Samuel 8–12 present two national leaders, Samuel *and* Saul, both of them depicted in terms connected to the era of the warrior–saviors,[60] despite the parallel between Judges 2:11–18 and 1 Samuel 7:3–4 delimiting the era. This does not suggest that the era of the book of Judges continues until 1 Samuel 12. Instead, it reflects the degree to which the conflict between figures like Saul and figures like Samuel clashed in the days before the monarchy was firmly established in earnest by David, and the weight of this recollection affected the Deuteronomists as they created their historiography. Behind the deliberate rhetoric of this historiography, however, is the evidence of the earlier traditions that show Saul claiming cultic hegemony and attempting to wrest this power away from the priesthood as he built his kingdom.

Such a wresting of power would involve a realignment of kinship organization. The previous trustees of the cult—Levite priests such as Samuel—had fought to maintain a position as inter-group interlocutors, thereby maintaining a *lateral* balance between these groups. The pro-Saul narratives imply that Saul should be the new patron of the cult (1 Sam 10:13), but not as an unbiased interlocutor between equal lineage groups. Rather, and as made explicit at the outset of the narrative, Saul was tightly bound to a Benjaminite chiefdom, which would have helmed a subordinate kinship hierarchy.[61] If Saul's chiefdom was expanded into a monarchic proto-state, such a state would have intensified and expanded that hierarchical structure, echoing the patrimonial dynamics of older Canaanite monarchic society.[62] In essence, the monarchy would have seen the Benjaminites, and Saul's clan in particular, in a privileged position.

Saul's leaning in this direction is evident within 1 Samuel 22: rather than priests being above and beyond kinship structures, Saul's order to have the priests of Nob slaughtered presupposes much older praxes where subordinate members of the royal "house" were dispatched in like manner for disloyalty to their sovereign.[63] The fulfillment of Samuel's anti-monarchic oracle in 1 Samuel 8:11–18 appears to have begun with Saul's reign, for between Saul's background as a chieftain and the adoption of pre-Israelite patrimonial expectations in the founding of his kingdom, the standards of Late Bronze Age kingship had once again crept back into the social world of the highland communities.

We have seen that it was against this idea that later biblical compositions such as the Pentateuchal legal collections and the prophetic invectives contend. At least in some sectors, the allergy toward monarchic patrimonial hierarchies was alive and well throughout (and likely beyond) the pre-exilic period. We have also seen that the same concept is implied in the closing chapter of the book of Judges, where the Shiloh sanctuary is said to be in the land of "Canaan," a land populated by a lawless, chaotic rabble by the end of the book. It is this type of cultural climate, the Deuteronomists argue, that was brought to an end by Samuel as they redacted his traditions to connect to the era of the judges. But it is also this cultural climate whence Saul came, and it is upon this model of authority that he built his realm.

The problem facing the Deuteronomistic redactors was immense. Even though David was the founder of the enduring dynasty, Saulides appear to have survived down to the time of the Deuteronomists' activity.[64] By this time, in fact, the Saulides faced an advantageous set of circumstances, for they stood blameless for the pitfalls involving Assyria that had befallen Israel under the watch of David's descendants in the 8th and 7th centuries BCE and which led to socio-economic and political calamities. The aforementioned problems associated with Saul's model of kingship may well have been remote from the minds of Judahites still reeling from the effects of the Assyrian crisis of the late 8th century, a crisis caused by the Davidide Hezekiah and his attempt to resist Assyrian hegemony.[65]

Many scholars make the case that the survival of the traditions regarding Saul as Israel's first king provided a potent alternative to the perceived failings of the Davidic line, and that this alternative royal line received support once Davidic power had been compromised.[66] It is no accident that following the demolition of Jerusalem in 587 BCE, it is the Benjaminite city of Mizpah, the place where Samuel publicly selected Saul to be Israel's king, which served as an administrative center under Babylonion rule.[67] It is similarly notable that the majority of the non-exiled population fled to the region of Benjamin—Saul's tribal homeland—following the Babylonian conquest of Judah, and remained there for the duration of the neo-Babylonian period.[68] The early to mid 6th century must have seen a renaissance of Saulide tradition among the populations seeking suitable representatives under Babylonian (or later, Persian) hegemony, and the questionable standing of the Davidides from the late 8th century onward certainly created space for the Saulides to emerge as a viable option during this time.[69]

The Deuteronomists clearly recognized that Saul's form of kingship derived from the same chieftain typology that characterized the pre-monarchic period. This not only tainted the institution of Israelite kingship, it clashed with the bias towards Levitical interests in the

Deuteronomistic tradition. It is, in fact, the Levitical predilections of these works that explain why the Deuteronomists stopped short of flat out rejecting kingship in Deuteronomy and why they upheld David as a royal standard throughout the book of Kings. The Levites had cast their lot with the David as a way of preserving their own self-interests during the early days of the monarchy. The turbulence of Absalom's revolt sees Levites maintaining strict allegiance to David; in that earlier period, an abandonment of David would impugn their numinous status following their affirmation of David as YHWH's chosen *nagid*.[70] As these Levites' ideological heirs, the Deuteronomists retained this sense of Davidic allegiance, even in the face of their desire to subordinate the royal office to sacral authority.

The redactors' solution was as radical as it was effective: playing upon the semantic range of the term *šophet*, and once again playing upon his liminal characteristics, the Levite–prophet Samuel was cast as the "last" judge. Through the tales of his leadership, the lawless era of the judges was brought to an end before the era of the monarchy even began. Indeed, the foundational pro-Saul texts that draw from the hallmarks of the judges traditions (1 Sam 9–11) are framed first by a Levitical–prophetic critique of the monarchic institution (1 Sam 8) and then by a Levitical–prophetic valedictory speech delimiting the terms of legitimate monarchic conduct (1 Sam 12)[71] and categorizing Samuel with judges of the past (1 Sam 12:11). These chapters effectively isolate the Saul narratives from the preceding material and simultaneously qualify it under a Levite/prophetic rhetorical rubric. Immediately thereafter, the annalistic formula from the book of Kings initiating the account of each monarch's reign was interpolated into the account of Saul's own reign (1 Sam 13:1, which is unfortunately textually corrupt in its current form), furthering the distinction between his form of governance and that which Samuel had brought to fulfillment in 1 Samuel 7.[72]

In sum

The end result of the foregoing is that kingship is divorced from chieftainship, which freed the Deuteronomists to re-invent it as an office licensed by Moses in Deuteronomy (Deut 17:14–20) that was expected to defer to sacral authority. Simultaneously, Samuel's juridical authority as a Levite and prophet was adapted to bring to an end the era of the judges by virtue of the semantic possibilities inherent in the term *šophet*. The redaction of the Deborah and Gideon traditions (Judg 4:4–5; 6:8–10) provided antecedents to Samuel's own status as a prophet in an attempt to establish a continuous prophetic line during the era of the judges down to Samuel's own day.[73] But this ultimately accomplished something of great value for the Deuteronomists. It created a literary universe where YHWH's covenantal law from Horeb, mediated through YHWH's prophetic servants, was always the highest law of the land under which all leaders were to operate. It was to this law that later audiences, confronted with social uncertainty and political turbulence, should cast their allegiance, following in the footsteps of national heroes such as Samuel who upheld its covenantal principles.

Conclusion

Samuel in Biblical and Extra-Biblical Perspective

> Follow men's eyes as they look to the skies
> The shifting shafts of shining weave the fabric of their dreams...
> —Rush, "Jacob's Ladder"

The previous chapters' analyses of Samuel's diverse characteristics lead to some important conclusions not only regarding the character of Samuel himself, but of conceptual trends running through ancient Israelite religion. Especially evident is the overlap between the Levitical, prophetic, and juridical responsibilities emerging in the Samuel traditions, which converge to create a literary meta-type. In Samuel, a much broader standard of leadership is established which traverses the boundaries between traditional offices, reframing and reshaping how the traditions surrounding those offices were perceived. This does not obtain solely in the Deuteronomistic History: in what follows, we will briefly survey texts from the Persian, Hellenistic, and Roman periods that utilize this composite Samuel to shape the diverse worldviews they each espouse.

Samuel in the Persian period sources

The phenomenon of prophecy seems to be a recurring vehicle for legitimacy exploited by the Jewish population of Persian Yehud in different ways. Subtle are the allusions to prophetic typologies embedded in Ezra–Nehemiah, especially with the characterization of Ezra himself. Ezra's words resonate with the Deuteronomic language regarding prophecy (Ezra 8:15–20; cf. Deut 18:15–18) and with the oracles of Jeremiah (Ezra 9:11–12; cf. Jer 29:5–7),[1] but the leadership typology of Ezra follows that of Samuel. Like Samuel, Ezra is of a priestly lineage (Ezra 7:1–5), functions as a scribe (Ezra 7:6; cf. 1 Sam 10:25), and intercedes on behalf of the people to YHWH (Ezra 9; cf. 1 Sam 7:5–12; 12:19–23). Moreover, just as Samuel establishes the parameters of the secular office of the king (1 Sam 8; 12), so too does Ezra lay the sacral foundations (in his capacity as a priest/scribe/law-giver) for the policies enacted by the layman Nehemiah, who follows him within the canonical sequence of Ezra–Nehemiah.[2] The implication is that just as Samuel heralded kingship, so does Ezra herald Nehemiah as both a trustee of national interest and as the direct representative of the Persian court.

Though the redaction of Ezra–Nehemiah was roughly contemporaneous to the redaction of Chronicles,[3] the Chronicler takes a very different view of the Samuel tradition and its applicability to life under Persian hegemony. Rather than using Samuel as a vehicle for incorporating Persian administration into Jewish religious consciousness, the Chronicler directs his audience away from external imperial fixtures and toward their own authentic religious institutions. This was no doubt influenced by the political turbulence between Persia and Greece in the mid to late 4th century BCE, which must have evoked diverse reactions from different factions in Jerusalem faced with the uncertainty of the outcome.[4] The Chronicler seems to have adopted an attitude different than the very pro-Persian redactors of Ezra–Nehemiah: for the Chronicler, the temple is the institution that binds together and defines Jewish identity, not Persian rulers or their regional representatives.[5] It is telling, though, that in depicting the organization of its priestly faculty, credit is shared by both David and Samuel:

All these [which were] chosen to be porters in the gates [were] two hundred and twelve. These were reckoned by their genealogy in their villages, whom David and Samuel the seer did ordain in their set office. (1 Chr 9:22)

Recent studies of the Chronicler's genealogies have revealed that the families and lineages included into these lists related to kinship networks of the Chronicler's own day, many of whom were no doubt marginalized by the exclusionary social politics reflected in Ezra–Nehemiah.[6] The Chronicler re-incorporates these populations back into his greater Israel by writing their lineages into the very origins of the Jerusalem temple in the golden age of David's reign. This makes the case that the temple standing in his day is not just a building sponsored by the Persian emperor, but was the legacy of all who trace their heritage to pre-exilic Israel ruled by Davidides.[7] But lest his audience view this as potentially limiting due to the fall of the Davidic dynasty, the Chronicler specifies that prophetic initiative stood—and indeed stands—behind the connection of these groups to the temple community. More intriguing, then, is the next reference to Samuel in the book of Chronicles:

Therefore came all the elders of Israel to the king to Hebron; and David made a covenant with them in Hebron before YHWH; and they anointed David king over Israel, according to the word of YHWH by Samuel. (1 Chr 11:3)

In the source for this passage, 2 Samuel 3, the elders come to David of their own volition and affirm him as king over all Israel with no mention made of Samuel. In the Chronicler's retelling of the event, however, the encounter between the elders and David occurs "according to the word of YHWH by Samuel," i.e., in accordance with a prophetic oracle or command voiced by Samuel. By the time of David's coronation in Hebron, Samuel has long since been dead, so this cannot be a contemporaneous order communicated by Samuel, but there is no previous text where Samuel offers such a directive to be carried outlater. Rather, the Chronicler may be directing his readers to consider the older sources in Samuel–Kings and their implications for the foundations of the Davidic monarchy as part of a prophetic plan for national existence. The temple plans drawn up by David in the subsequent chapters, then, are extensions of that plan and move beyond the category of royal institution.

The Chronicler also invokes Samuel in his retelling of one of the most pivotal moments in the book of Kings and thus one of central memories of pre-exilic Israelite religion, namely, the Passover festival that caps the account of Josiah's religious reform. The role that Samuel plays in the Chronicler's retelling of the Kings version is illuminating, and we shall therefore compare both texts:

And the king commanded all the people, saying, Keep the Passover to YHWH your God, as [it is] written in the book of this covenant. *Surely there was no such Passover from the days of the judges that judged Israel*, nor in all the days of the kings of Israel, nor of the kings of Judah; But in the eighteenth year of king Josiah, [wherein] this Passover was observed to YHWH in Jerusalem. (2 Kgs 23:21–3)

Moreover Josiah kept a Passover to YHWH in Jerusalem ... *And there was no Passover like that kept in Israel since the days of Samuel the prophet*; neither did all the kings of Israel keep such a Passover as Josiah kept, and the priests, and the Levites, and all Judah and Israel that were present, and the inhabitants of Jerusalem. (2 Chr 35:1, 18)

2 Chronicles 34–5 is famous for its assignment of detailed duties to Levites that the source material in Kings lacks, and this corresponds to the Chronicler's desire to link traditions and communities within the institution of the temple. The rhetorical importance of Samuel is essential to this effort in the Chronicler's purview, as the standards of Passover celebration are aligned with him and the prophetic tradition he symbolized over against the judges mentioned in the source material in Kings.[8] The monarchs and judges in the Scriptural sources the Chronicler inherited had lost credibility in the minds of his audience, and would serve little purpose in providing a stamp of theological authenticity. Samuel, however, still loomed large and was deemed a suitable replacement. Samuel's place as the prophetic guardian of the nation through the shift from one epoch to the next (the era of judges to that of monarchy) points ahead to the Chronicler's own composition serving a similar purpose as Greek threats to Persian imperial hegemony loomed in the distance.[9]

Samuel in the Hellenistic Jewish sources

As evidenced by the Chronicler's work, Samuel had become an iconic figure in early Jewish religious thought, suitable for the hermeneutical reframing of the past and advancing innovative theological concepts. This understanding is presupposed by important texts beyond the canon of the Hebrew Scriptures as well. The extra-canonical book of Ben Sira lavishes extensive praise upon Samuel in his famous "Praise of the Fathers" (Sir 44–50):[10]

Samuel was beloved by his Lord; a prophet of the Lord, he established the kingdom and anointed rulers over his people. By the law of the Lord he judged the congregation, and the Lord watched over Jacob. By his faithfulness he was proved to be a prophet, and by his words he became known as a trustworthy seer. He called upon the Lord, the Mighty One, when his enemies pressed him on every side, and he offered in sacrifice a suckling lamb. Then the Lord thundered from heaven, and made his voice heard with a mighty sound; he subdued the leaders of the enemy and all the rulers of the Philistines. Before the time of his eternal sleep, Samuel bore witness before the Lord and his anointed: "No property, not so much as a pair of shoes, have I taken from anyone!" And no one accused him. Even after he had fallen asleep, he prophesied and made known to the king his death, and lifted up his voice from the ground in prophecy, to blot out the wickedness of the people. (Sir 46:13–20)

Commentators on Ben Sira note that the discourse on Samuel is part of a special category including Moses, Joshua, David, Hezekiah, and Josiah: common lexical formulae are applied to all five of these figures, combining with overlapping motifs in setting them apart from other luminaries in Ben Sira's list, resulting in what Jeremy Corley has termed "canonical assimilation."[11] That is, qualities from the older sources regarding each figure are projected onto the others, and lemmas in the once-discreet textual sources are shared by all as evidence of a growing canon of Scripture. Given Ben Sira's sympathies for the priesthood of his day and the high priest Simeon II in particular (Sir 50:1–21), Ben Sira's interest in this group emerges more clearly. The roost of Simeon II was a temple whose origins are traced in earlier tradition to David, so the highlighting of David and kings who reportedly centralized the cult therein (Hezekiah and Josiah) is to be expected. And since this temple was the intellectual and geographical locus of the teaching of the *torah* of Moses, the inclusion of Moses is obvious. Why, however, is a figure such as Aaron—the "founding" figure of the Jerusalem priesthood deemed worthy of extensive praise (Sir 45:6–22)—left out of this special category, and why would Joshua and Samuel be included and typologically merged, as Corley observes?

An answer lies in Corley's observation that Ben Sira recalls Samuel's prophetic authority as a forerunner to that of Simeon II. Since both Joshua and Samuel are included in this particular category and features of each are assimilated into each other, the connection to Simeon II must go beyond purely priestly ritual conduct.[12] As we have seen, both Joshua and Samuel complete the charge to carry out a *herem* against an outsider group in defining the political and ethnic boundaries of Israel. This purpose of the *herem* conducted by each figure would not have been lost on Ben Sira, since question of social boundary marking is of particular interest to him. This is evident, for example, in his favoring of Nehemiah (Sir 49:13)—who successfully separates his countrymen from "foreigners" and constructs a wall around Jerusalem as a monument to this accomplishment—over Ezra, whose memoir ends without resolving the problem of foreign marriage and who consequently receives no mention in Ben Sira's writings. Ben Sira's emphasis on Samuel, then, may have less to do with the latter's ritual actions and more to do with how, as the outstanding priest of his day, he successfully delineated the boundaries between Israel and foreign nations such as Amalek during turbulent times.

Since Ben Sira dates to ca. 190 BCE, his writings must be viewed in the wake of the transition from Ptolemaic to Seleucid hegemony over Judah (201 BCE).[13] During this time much uncertainty must have surfaced regarding the fate of the Jewish population therein, both in terms of political fortunes and theological integrity. Ben Sira's engagement of Hellenistic thought testifies to his cosmopolitan enculturation as a scribe and, as some have suggested, as a member of a priesthood that mediated between the Jewish people and the (by then) relatively familiar Ptolemies. Yet to connect Simeon II to a character like Samuel—a priest who maintained the nation's ethnic boundaries through the *herem* like Joshua, who was credited with planning the Jerusalem Temple with David, and who followed in the footsteps of Moses as a prophet—suggests that he, and not other pretenders to political power, could be trusted to maintain the religious and social distinctiveness of the Jewish world in the face of an untested Seleucid "other."[14]

That this very issue is taken up by the authors of Daniel less than a generation later (ca.165 BCE) and with a much increased measure of anxiety regarding foreign empires indicates that the era saw a rising need to seek refuge in the past. Ben Sira's choice to cast Simeon II as a sort of Samuel *redivivus* testifies to the prominent place Samuel had obtained as a *topos* of cultural and religious identity by the Hellenistic period. As Alex Jassen has discussed in his recent study of the so-called "Samuel Apocryphon" at Qumran (4Q 160), this understanding of Samuel survived down into the Hasmonean period. The sectarian faction represented by this text saw fit to recast 1 Samuel 3 as the context for a prayer, placed in Samuel's mouth, composed to appeal for protection against forces within the Jewish world that heralded corruption and danger.[15] Jassen is on target when he observes that "Samuel is chosen as the pseudepigraphic voice for this prayer on account of the biblical and post-biblical tradition that identifies him as the petitioner *par excellence* on behalf of Israel."[16] However, given the polarizing tone pervasive in the Qumran literature, the boundary-marking qualities attributed to Samuel must also play into the choice to recruit this character to the authors' cause. The distinction between Ben Sira and 4Q 160 in their respective usages of Samuel is that the former appears to build upon Samuel's shoulders a distinction between the Jewish world and the Seleucid world, while the latter narrows the scope of the Jewish world to the sectarian group standing behind that work and uses Samuel to qualify opposing Jewish groups as the "other."

Samuel in Roman period Jewish works

Yet if the Hellenistic sources suggest that Samuel was used as a vehicle to create boundaries between Jewish communities and the world beyond them, the Jewish writers of the Roman era appear to utilize him for opposite purposes. Josephus, for instance, devotes more elaborate attention to Samuel than to any other prophet,[17] and repeatedly refers to him overtly as "prophet" over against the relatively few times this title appears in the biblical sources. Josephus' amplification of Samuel's prophetic title and function and the liberties he takes in departing from the biblical source material are meant to suggest that the features of society from Josephus' day that had maintained stability within the Jewish world and between Jews and Romans were already in place in Samuel's time. Telling, for example, is Josephus' portrayal of the *bamah* banquet scene from 1 Samuel 9:20, where the number of people in attendance is exactly seventy (*Ant* 6.52); counting Samuel as the president of this event, the number comes to seventy-one. Parallels have been drawn between this passage and the institution of the Sanhedrin (whose members also numbered seventy-one with the high priest of Jerusalem presiding over it),[18] but this is not simply a matter of conventional expression on Josephus' part. Rather, the flourish suggests that the Sanhedrin existed even before the temple was built by King Solomon and even before the reign of Saul, Israel's first king.

Louis Feldman has argued that this contributes to Josephus' view that theocracy was the ideal form of governance,[19] and Samuel is elsewhere utilized by Josephus as a platform for political and philosophical speculation and declarations meant to suggest that Judaism—even its oldest phases—was compatible with Roman imperialism. The Sanhedrin had been a more potent tool for Roman governance of the Jewish world than the remnants of the local royal dynasties in Judea, for Jews even beyond Judea cast allegiance to the leadership in the Jerusalem temple and not to the wisps of the former Hasmomean line or the Herodian rulers. But following the destruction of the temple (70 CE), questions invariably arose regarding where Jewish political loyalties would fall.

Josephus' rendition of the Samuel narratives informs his Roman audience that Jews would continue to be loyal subjects of Rome. As his example of Samuel demonstrates, they were naturally and originally predisposed toward theocratic leadership, with kingship only secondarily emerging and holding a subsidiary position. The depiction of Samuel as helming a Sanhedrin-like conclave, for example, bolsters this position. Josephus makes the case that the ideology undergirding the Sanhedrin (theocratic leadership working in the interests of the Judean *Pax Romana*) was a deeply entrenched Jewish sensibility that did not need a Jerusalem temple in order to survive, and which could continue to facilitate Jewish–Roman relations through the proper channels of Jewish social leadership—doubtlessly, figures such as Josephus himself, who possessed priestly heritage on the one hand and Roman citizenship on the other.

The special attention given to the Samuel tradition in making this case and the case for compatibility more generally is to be attributed to Josephus' pragmatism: Samuel was a hero from the past, but the Scriptural record situates him in a setting that is primarily tangible rather than mythic. The values he represents and actualizes, Josephus suggests, were not disconnected from the slings and arrows of *Realpolitik*, but emerged from the affairs of state. Yet Josephus' version of the Samuel tale, with its decidedly elitist–political interests, contrasts with that of his near-contemporary Pseudo-Philo, who utilizes the Samuel tradition as a platform for demonstrating Jewish uniqueness within the Roman imperial world in his work *Liber Antiquitatum Biblicarum* (*LAB*).[20] Though the narrative of Samuel's birth and youth is sprinkled with conventional flourishes found in contemporaneous non-Jewish narratives,[21] Jews within the pagan world are charged with a responsibility that retains their identity through interfacing with surrounding peoples, as evident in the re-telling of Hannah's thanksgiving prayer from 1 Samuel 2:1–10:

> Come ye at my voice, all ye peoples, and give ear unto my speech, all ye kingdoms, for my mouth is opened that I may speak, and my lips are commanded that I may sing praises unto the Lord. Drop, O my breasts, and give forth your testimonies, for it is appointed to you to give suck. For he shall be set up that is suckled by you, *and by his words shall the people be enlightened*, and he shall show unto the nations their boundaries, and his horn shall be greatly exalted. (*LAB* 51.3–4)

The note that "by his words shall the people be enlightened" draws from Isaiah 51:4, a passage composed when Israel lived as one of many nations ruled by Persia.[22] Even if Pseudo-Philo did not recognize this compositional setting, the verses' thematic thrust and impact was obviously deemed appropriate for his compositional purposes. The retelling of the Samuel narratives in *LAB* allows for greater contact between Israel and foreigners, promoting a theology that maintains Israel's connection to its deity, but one that does not take place in a socio-cultural vacuum. Samuel's prophetic role benefits Israel by expanding the parameters of his authority to speak as an inter-ethnic figure. Like Josephus, then, Pseudo-Philo uses Samuel to set the Jewish people within their multinational imperial milieu, and like Josephus, he goes on to criticize Israelite kingship as inferior to theocratic leadership. But unlike Josephus, who seems primarily concerned with how the heirs to Samuel might interact with their imperial superiors, Pseudo-Philo creates a Samuel narrative that interfaces Judaism's neighboring cultures, and suggests that Judaism should administer divine *torah* to the nations—as a challenge to Roman authority.[23]

Samuel in Rabbinic and Christian texts

The rabbinic traditions about Samuel synthesize many of the diverse biblical texts in which his name appears. The Rabbis accepted his status as a judge and priest (*LevR* xxii 6; *NumR* xviii 17; *Berakhot* 31b; *Ta'anit* 5b) but, like both Josephus and Pseudo-Philo, devoted special attention to his prophetic status. And like Josephus and Pseudo-Philo, Samuel's prophetic authority is shaped to promote the interests of the Rabbis, as his prophetic authority is demonstrated through his exegesis of Scripture and hermeneutical method. A 3rd–century CE sage, Rabbi Eleazar b. Pedath, is credited with transmitting the following tradition:

> Samuel was guilty of giving a decision in the presence of his teacher; for it says, And when the bullock was slain, the child was brought to Eli. Because the bullock was slain, did they bring the child to Eli? What it means is this. Eli said to them: Call a priest and let him come and kill [the animal]. When Samuel saw them looking for a priest to kill it, he said to them, Why do you go looking for a priest to kill it? The shechitah may be performed by a layman! They brought him to Eli, who asked him, How do you know this? He replied: Is it written, 'The priest shall kill'? It is written, The priests shall present [the blood]: the office of the priest begins with the receiving of the blood, which shows that shechitah may be performed by a layman. He said to him: You have spoken very well, but all the same you are guilty of giving a decision in the presence of your teacher, and whoever gives a decision in the presence of his teacher is liable to the death penalty. Thereupon Hannah came and cried before him: 'I am the woman that stood by thee here etc.'. He said to her: Let me punish him and I will pray to God and He will give thee a better one than this. She then said to him: 'For this child I prayed'. (*Berakhot* 31b)

This passage draws from the authoritative biblical sources in 1 Samuel 1–3 that reveal the rivalry between Samuel and the Elides, but new dimensions are added to it. The Talmud preserves indications that wisdom—one of the hallmarks of a rabbinic sage's authority—was already a quality that separated Samuel from his predecessor Eli (*Shabbat* 113b), but in our passage, Samuel demonstrates his fitness for leadership through traditional methods of rabbinic argumentation. His statement that laypeople may sacrifice affirms the ruling in

Zebakhim 32a that a layperson is permitted to conduct sacrificial slaughter,[24] but the passage goes on to provide a proof for this ruling by applying it to the cult at Shiloh.

The circle of authorship or school of thought aligned with *Zebakhim* 32a may therefore stand behind the episode in Berakhot 31b, but the latter moves the discussion beyond the realm of legal theory and into that of polemics characterizing the post-70 CE social landscape. Despite the 3rd century date of the tale's purported transmitter, the tradition it enshrines likely possesses earlier origins.[25] The populist bent coupled with the cultic emphasis of *Berakhot* 31b suggest an old tradition rooted in Pharisaic circles,[26] and the particular logic utilized to challenge priestly conduct is based on the Hillelite hermeneutical rules of *binyan 'ab* (application of a provision from an authoritative source) and *dabar ha-lamed me-'inyano* (deduction from context).[27] But the real focus of the passage is on the draconian inclinations of Eli, who is unwilling to accept a credible legal observation from a student and who consequently proclaims death as a just punishment. The rabbis maintained the authority of teachers but supported the viability of a new insight produced by a subsequent student, and this process was deemed integral to the sustenance of *torah*.[28]

That Eli is pitted against Samuel as a threat not only to him but the rabbinic concepts placed in his mouth points to a tension that existed between the rabbinic movement on the one hand and the remnants of the Jerusalem temple priesthood on the other. The latter had, of course, lost considerable power following the destruction of the temple in 70 CE, but there is much evidence beyond rabbinic texts that priests continued to assert themselves as communal authorities.[29] *Berakhot* 31b makes a counterclaim: Samuel was not a forerunner to the post-70 CE priests but a forerunner to the Rabbis. His supersession of the Elides after the destruction of Shiloh parallels and anticipates the supersession of the Rabbis over the Jerusalem priesthood after the destruction of the temple.

The deployment of Samuel as a surrogate for the Rabbis is found elsewhere as well. In particular, parallels appear between Samuel and the growing office of the Patriarch, the force behind the codification of the Mishnah (ca. 200 CE) and the patron of the rabbinic movement in the Galilee by the 4th century.[30] The office of the Patriarch was taken up by Jewish elites who possessed wealth, who were cosmopolitan in nature, and who expanded their influence into the synagogues of surrounding communities via rabbinic agency (though the rabbinic movement found greater influence following the demise of the office of the Patriarch).[31] Samuel is cast in similar shades: he is depicted as possessing great wealth, commanding a large entourage when he travelled, and committed to disseminating religious doctrine throughout the countryside (*Berakhot* 10b; 31b; *Ta'anit* 5b).

The Palestinian Talmud (mid 5th century CE) goes so far as to use the same terminology for Samuel that was used for Judah the Patriarch: he is "the *rabban*, the great master," teacher of all the prophets (PT *Hag* 77a). Especially significant, though, is the tradition that Samuel's merit exceeded even that of Moses by virtue of how revelation was secured by each. Moses secured revelation by approaching God in the Tabernacle, whereas God came to Samuel at Shiloh and beyond (*ExodR* xvi 4). If indeed the Jerusalem priesthood had laid claim to "the torah of Moses" as the text they were solely empowered to teach, then Rabbis active after the temple's destruction would be well served to position Samuel—Moses' equal in other respects—as superior by virtue of his *dissociation* from a single, central cult site and his dissemination of *torah* throughout the land.

The tale of Samuel's *halakhic* challenge to the Elides has a strong parallel in the Gospel according to Luke, where it is the young Jesus who is a learned scholar of *halakha* (binding ritual/legal practice) in the presence of the priests:

Every year Jesus' parents went to Jerusalem for the Festival of the Passover. When he was twelve years old, they went up to the festival, according to the custom. After the festival was over, while his parents were returning home, the boy Jesus stayed behind in Jerusalem, but they were unaware of it. Thinking he was in their company, they traveled on for a day. Then they began looking for him among their relatives and friends. When they did not find him, they went back to Jerusalem to look for him. After three days they found him in the temple courts, sitting among the teachers, listening to them and asking them questions. Everyone who heard him was amazed at his understanding and his answers... And Jesus grew in wisdom and stature, and in favor with God and man. (Luke 2:41–7, 52)

The passage above is consistent with the work of other New Testament writers who recognized and validated Samuel's important place in the pantheon of prophets in the Hebrew Scriptures.[32] There are several overlaps here and elsewhere in Luke's account of Jesus' youth with the narrative in 1 Samuel 1–3, but it is important that the primary thrust in the passage above engages the picture of Samuel not from the Hebrew Scriptures, but from the rabbinic tradition in *Berakhot* 31b. Both Samuel and Jesus are precocious in their legal insight, and both demonstrate these skills in cultic contexts, suggesting the eventual replacement of ritual with exegesis and intellectual speculation in a post-temple environment. It is unclear if one tradition directly inspired the other, though the points of contact elsewhere in Luke 1–2 with 1 Samuel 1–3 could be used to support the view that the Lukan author has appropriated an older Jewish tradition regarding Samuel in his characterization of Jesus, and it is clear that Luke interacts with older Pharisaic tradition intimately.[33]

This does not fundamentally differ, however, from the purpose of 1 Samuel 1–3 as discussed in chapter 2 of the present study. In that narrative, Samuel is equated with Moses by virtue of Mosaic language and imagery for the purposes of usurping a Mushite priestly order that had lost its luster. In Luke, Jesus is equated with Samuel by virtue of language and imagery associated with the latter for similar purposes, and it is notable that not only is material from the Hebrew Scriptures recruited for this task, but, if Luke 2:41–52 knows and draws from the tradition beneath *Berakhot* 31b, oral rabbinic lore as well.[34] Just as the authors of 1 Samuel 1–3 sought to sideline Mushite claims to exclusive authority over the Israelite cult, so too does the Lukan author attempt to sideline rabbinic claims to exclusive authority regarding the interpretation of the Hebrew Scriptures. It is not through the hands of the Rabbis, who ostensibly follow the lead of Samuel, that one may discern the meaning of the divine word. Rather, it is through the disciples of Jesus, who follow an equally authoritative model (ergo the parallels with *Berakhot* 31b) but one distinct from that fostered by the Rabbis (ergo the transfer of the tradition from Samuel to Jesus), that the meaning of the Hebrew Scriptures may be best understood.

This brief passage speaks to a wider rhetorical strategy in the early Christian writings regarding the place of Jesus as the liminal figure *par excellence*: it is Jesus who mediates between communities throughout the Mediterranean and Asia Minor, and it is through him that a new quasi-ethnos is created in the space between Jew and Greek (Gal 3:28; Col 3:11). It is Jesus who mediates between the old Hebrew Scriptures and the new terms of covenantal existence (Mat 5), and it is he who contends against the forces of cosmic evil in the wilderness and who embodies the victorious outcome of that conflict upon his return to the civilized world (Mat 4; Luke 4). Most significantly—as both the Son of God and as the Son of Man—it is he who embodies the portal between heaven and earth, the event horizon between the realm of the divine and the realm of mortality.

With this new paradigm, the legacy of Samuel's own liminality was irrevocably altered in the growth of Christian tradition. Samuel became one of many exponents of a persistent divine word that found ultimate fulfillment in the mission, teachings, and person of Jesus. As such, he (Samuel) was part of a definitive *standard* of tradition now subject to redefinition and requalification. Yet Samuel's liminality survives and contributes to that of Jesus not only by virtue of the application of the *Berakhot* 31b Samuel tradition to the Lukan context, but by Jesus' own admission that his teachings stand in complete consistency with the words of the prophets who came before him. Jesus inherits and amplifies not only the words of prophets like Samuel, but his location on both the social and cosmic continuum, standing between creator and community just as Samuel did, though possessing unprecedented genetic connections to both.

In sum

The use of Samuel as a rhetorical *topos* in texts beginning with Chronicles and persisting into the rabbinic period may achieve the same legitimizing ends as the earlier Deuteronomistic and pre-Deuteronomistic texts, but there is a crucial difference. The earlier compositions derived from a time when Israelite religion still resonated with the idea of socio-political independence. In the eyes of pre-exilic Israel, they were a nation set aside from all other nations to be YHWH's treasured possession, a people surrounded by foreign cultures whose social horizons extended to the boundaries of their own land. The experience of the Babylonian exile changed this, and writers of the later texts have in turn shed these illusions. For them, Israel's social horizons were international, indeed universal; the encounter with empire after empire, century after century reinforced this understanding. Their connection to YHWH was therefore expanded in kind to possess an international scope, and as such the cumulative traditions that defined them were viewed as central and edifying in world history. With this international sensibility, the significance of appeals to Samuel underwent an important change. He no longer only mediated between Israelite/Jewish social types, but became symbolic of an entire religious heritage utilized to set Jewish tradition within—or against—outsider groups. Yet in some ways, continuity between past and present was preserved as these authors placed Samuel at the boundary between their own communities and the larger world beyond them. In this way, Samuel remained liminal, facilitating the interface between disparate ideologies as communities continued to re-define themselves and shape their own traditions of identity.

Notes

INTRODUCTION

1. By "book of Samuel," I refer to the canonical books 1–2 Samuel.
2. On the breakdown of chapters concerned with Saul or David as reflecting the dominance of the latter's dynasty in the formation of the biblical narrative, see Carol Meyers, "Kinship and Kingship: The Early Monarchy," *The Oxford History of Biblical Israel* (ed. Michael D. Coogan; New York/Oxford: Oxford University Press, 1998) 171.
3. See Marsha C. White "'The History of Saul's Rise': Saulide State Propaganda in 1 Samuel 1–14', *"A Wise And Discerning Mind": Essays in Honor of Burke O. Long* (ed. Saul M. Olyan and Robert C. Culley, BJS; Providence: Brown University, 2000) 287–8; Robert Polzin, *Samuel and the Deuteronomist* (San Francisco: Harper and Row, 1989) 22–6; Reinhard G. Kratz, *The Composition of the Narrative Books of the Old Testament* (London: T & T Clark, 2005) 174; P. Kyle McCarter, *I Samuel* (AB; Garden City: Doubleday, 1980) 65; and Marc Zvi Brettler, *The Creation of History in Ancient Israel* (London: Routledge, 1995) 109; Jan Dus, "Die Geburtslegende Samuels, I Sam 1: Eine traditionsgeschichtliche Untersuchung zu 1 Sam 1–3," *Revista degli Studi Orientali* 43 (1968) 163–94; Joseph Blenkinsopp, *A History of Prophecy in Israel* (Louisville: Westminster John Knox, 1996) 52–3; they all argue that an originally Saulide birth narrative was overwritten to apply to Samuel.
4. The most recent and thorough analysis of these materials originating in the context of royal propaganda is that of Jeremy M. Hutton, *The Transjordanian Palimpsest: The Overwritten Texts of Personal Exile and Transformation in the Deuteronomistic History* (BZAW; Berlin: De Gruyter, 2009) especially 364–71. See also William M. Schniedewind, *Society and the Promise to David* (New York/Oxford: Oxford University Press, 1999) 23–4. For a valuable overview of the book of Samuel as historiographic literature and a suggestion regarding its importance as an historical resource even as a work laden with ideological agenda, see Rachelle Gilmour, *Representing The Past: A Literary Analysis of Narrative Historiography in the Book of Samuel* (VTSup; Leiden/Boston: Brill, 2011) 1–33.

5. Frank Moore Cross, *Canaanite Myth and Hebrew Epic* (Cambridge, MA: Harvard University Press, 1973) 223.
6. Positions on the date and provenance of this narrative range dramatically. Diana V. Edelman views this as part of a late 7th century Deuteronomistic composition (*King Saul in the Historiography of Judah* [JSOTSup; Sheffield: Sheffield Academic Press, 1991]). White ("The History of Saul's Rise," 284–7, 291–2) and Hutton (*The Transjordanian Palimpsest*, 365) both argue for the origins of this narrative in a much earlier period among pro-Saul circles, though their breakdown of this narrative and their proposals regarding the growth of the narrative in which it appears differ significantly.
7. Jonathan Jacobs, "The Role of the Secondary Characters in the Story of the Anointing of Saul (1 Samuel ix–x)," *VT* 58 (2008) 499–506.
8. See the comments by W. H. C. Propp, *Exodus 19–40* (AB; New York: Doubleday, 2006) 297–8 regarding the covenant meal between the elders and YHWH at Sinai. See also Katherine Roberts, "God, Prophet, and King: Eating and Drinking on the Mountain in First Kings 18:41," *CBQ* 62 (2000) 631–44 for the ritual meal affirming Ahab's royal viability. The ritual meal is part of an archaic near eastern mythic pattern; see Paul D. Hanson, "Zechariah 9 and the Recapitulation of an Ancient Ritual Pattern," *JBL* 92 (1973) 52–3.
9. Serge Frolov notes that the meal served to Saul during the banquet is connected to foodstuffs in the Pentateuch associated with priesthood ("The Semiotics of Covert Action in 1 Sam 9–10," *JSOT* 31.4 [2007] 433 n. 8). His position that the entire event is a cloak-and-dagger resistance episode, however, does not account for the use of Samuel as a propagandistic legitimizing factor in the construction of the Saulide traditions (as per White, "Saul's Rise," 291–2).
10. In W. Beyerlin's view, this episode declares a new standard of charisma for Saul as the king-elect that previous leaders in the book of Judges did not possess ("Das Königscharisma bei Saul," *ZAW* 73 [1961] 187–90).
11. On 1 Samuel 22 specifically, see White, "History of Saul's Rise," 291–2.
12. This narrative is often assigned to a redactional effort—the so-called "Prophetic Record"—dating from the mid to late 8th century BCE. See the discussion below for more on the Prophetic Record model. I do not dispute in principle the view that these verses may derive from a considerably later period than the early Saul narrative in 1 Samuel 9:1–10:16, but even if the authors of 1 Samuel 16:1–13 are part of a later prophetic group, they nevertheless pit David against Saul as a suitable king and thereby function as royal apologists in their own way.

13. Edelman, *King Saul*, 43–4. So also the implications of Christopher Hauer's discussion ("Does 1 Samuel 9:1–11:15 Reflect the Extension of Saul's Dominion?," *JBL* 86 [1967] 307–8).
14. On the sacral role of kin group elders, see Stephen L. Cook, *The Social Roots of Biblical Yahwism* (Atlanta: SBL, 2004) 205–14.
15. So also Halpern's observations regarding David's "ritual humility" at the point of his selection by Samuel (*David's Secret Demons*, 19).
16. Zechariah Kallai, "Biblical Historiography and Literary History; A Programmatic Survey," *VT* 49 (1999) 345.
17. As with the phrase "book of Samuel," my use of "the book of Chronicles" relates to the canonical text 1–2 Chronicles.
18. Hutton's recent analysis (*The Transjordanian Palimpsest*, 364–71 and *passim*) provides the most exhaustive and current treatment of these redactional layers. See also his review of the major scholarly positions in op. cit., 113–56. Hutton's study develops the model of a pre-Deuteronomistic "Prophetic Record" proposed by Antony F. Campbell (*Of Prophets and Kings: A Late Ninth-Century Document (1 Samuel 1–2 Kings 10)* [CBQMS; Washington D.C.: CBA, 1986] 101–3 [for a list of passages he ascribes to this source], 111–23) and McCarter (*I Samuel*, 18–23). See also Walter Dietrich's *The Early Monarchy in Israel: The Tenth Century BCE* (Atlanta: SBL, 2007; original, 1997), who similarly sees several early compositional layers pre-dating a comprehensive redaction in the late pre-exilic period. There are obviously views to the contrary: Kurt Noll, for example, assumes the book of Samuel to be a Hellenistic text virtually in its entirety ("Is The Scroll of Samuel Deuteronomistic?," paper presented at the 2011 Annual Meeting of the Society of Biblical Literature; idem, "Deuteronomistic History or Deuteronomistic Debate? (A Thought Experiment)" *JSOT* 313 [2007] 325–7, 336). Other scholars, however, see most of the book of Samuel deriving from an early (10th century) context with only very limited Deuteronomistic editing. See Moshe Garsiel, "The Book of Samuel: Its Composition, Structure and Significance as a Historiographical Source," *Journal of Hebrew Scriptures* 10 (2010) Article 5, 34–42 (http://www.jhsonline.org). Others look to major blocks of material in the book as obtaining in an early context. See David Toshio Tsumura, *The Royal Dynasties in Ancient Israel: A Study on the Formation and Development of Royal-Dynastic Ideology* (BZAW; Berlin: De Gruyter, 1977).
19. See, e.g., Ehud Ben Zvi, "Reconstructing the Intellectual Discourse of Ancient Yehud," *Studies in Religion* 39 (2010) 7–23; idem, "'The Prophets'—References to Generic Prophets and their Role in the Construction of the Image of the 'Prophets of Old' within the Postmonarchic

Readership/s of the Book of Kings," *ZAW* 116 (2004) 555–67 (especially pp. 565–6). Ben Zvi's view here has much in common with the observations of David M. Carr (*Writing on the Tablet of the Heart: Origins of Scripture and Literature* (New York/Oxford: Oxford University Press, 2005) and Raymond F. Person (*The Deuteronomistic History and the Book of Chronicles: Scribal Works in an Oral World* [Atlanta: SBL, 2010] 41–68) who emphasize the significance of the enculturation of scribes in an oral–textual social context.

20. On Psalm 99, see Mark Leuchter, "The Literary Strata and Narrative Sources of Psalm xcix," *VT* 55 (2005) 18–36.

21. For a discussion of the priest/prophet dichotomy that emerges by the time of the Jeremiah tradition, see chapter 2 of the present study. By the late 7th century, Moses and Samuel were regarded as prophets more than priests, but the author of Psalm 99 presumes priesthood as their outstanding quality.

22. Edelman, *King Saul*, 42, 69, 79–80; Keith Bodner, *1 Samuel: A Narrative Commentary* (Sheffield: Sheffield Phoenix Press, 2008) 71–2, 75, 113; Roy L. Heller, *Power, Politics and Prophecy: The Character of Samuel and the Deuteronomistic Evaluation of Prophecy* (London/New York: T & T Clark, 2006) 43.

23. Heller, *Power, Politics and Prophecy*, 150.

24. Pace Heller, op. cit. The diversity of prophetic types and phenomena one encounters in Samuel–Kings (and elsewhere) justifies Heller's view that the Deuteronomistic evaluation of prophecy is one that renders it a mysterious and ambiguous phenomenon (p. 150). However, as I hope to show in the ensuing chapters, the particularly Deuteronomistic brand of prophetic leadership that Samuel represents is identified as superior to other leadership types, even if Samuel himself is sometimes the recipient of tacit criticism.

25. Samuel's family connection is attested both in 1 Samuel 1–2 and in 1 Samuel 7:17; 9:4–10:9 (where he remains at his family's home in *'eretz zuph/ramathaim zophim*).

26. On the acephalous nature of pre-monarchic Israel, see Robert D. Miller, *Chieftains of the Highland Clans: A History of Israel in the Twelfth and Eleventh Centuries BC* (Grand Rapids: Eerdmans, 2005); James W. Flanagan, "Chiefs in Israel," *JSOT* 20 (1981) 47–73 (despite the differences between Miller and Flanagan in their view of the chiefdom/state transition, both studies provide useful information regarding the function of chieftains). See also Karel van der Toorn, *Family Religion in Babylonia, Syria and Israel* (Leiden: Brill, 1996) 190–205.

27. This clashes with the Hebrew word for "ask," ša'al, which contributes to the common view that 1 Samuel 1–2 relate to Saul at least as much as they do to Samuel; see chapter 2 of the present study for further discussion.

28. McCarter points to the explanation in 1 Samuel 1:20 as an attempt to explain the name as though it were šeme'el, "[he who is] from God," but that the original form of the name was more likely šem-uhu-'il, "his name is El" (*I Samuel*, 62).

29. Blenkinsopp, *A History of Prophecy*, 52.

30. The polarity between the sown and unsown and the role of liminal space is a very ancient fixture of Levantine mythology. See Mark S. Smith, *The Origins of Biblical Monotheism* (New York/Oxford: Oxford University Press, 2002) 27–9; Gregory Mobley, *Samson and the Liminal Hero in the Ancient Near East* (New York/London: T & T Clark, 2006). On liminality as a constitutive element in Israel's sense of its own origins, see Susan Ackerman, "Why Is Miriam Also Among The Prophets? (And Is Zipporah Among the Priests?)," *JBL* 121 (2002) 75–80.

31. On Canaanite origins, see William G. Dever, *Who Were The Early Israelites and Where Did They Come From?* (Grand Rapids: Eerdmans, 2003). On eastern nomadic heritage, see Kenton L. Sparks, "Israel and the Nomads of Ancient Palestine," *Community Identity in Judean Historiography* (ed. Gerald N. Knoppers and Kenneth A. Ristau; Winona Lake: Eisenbrauns, 2009) 19–26. See also J. David Scholen, "Caravans, Kenites, and *Casus Belli*: Enmity and Alliance in the Song of Deborah," *CBQ* 55 (1993) 33–8, who sees early Israel as an amalgam of sedentary highland dwellers and interconnected eastern nomadic groups. In my view, Schloen's perspective remains the most useful in accounting for diversity in early Israel, though the evidence that Dever marshals, coupled with the strong currents of Canaanite myth retained in the biblical tradition, must factor significantly into any proposed model of Israelite ethnogenesis.

32. On the theologizing/liturgizing of these social conditions, see Mark Leuchter, "Eisodus as Exodus: The Song of the Sea (Exod 15) Reconsidered," *Bib* 92 (2011) 333–6.

33. On the pre-Israelite association of YHWH with the wilderness and its attestation in ancient poetry, see Lawrence E. Stager, "Forging an Identity: The Emergence of Ancient Israel," *The Oxford History of the Biblical World*, 105–8.

34. Mobley, *Samson and the Liminal Hero*, 63–5; Mobley, *The Empty Men: The Heroic Tradition of Ancient Israel* (New York: Doubleday, 2005).

35. See Ronald Hendel, "The Exodus in Biblical Memory," *JBL* 120 (2001) 602–4, 615–20; Ronald Hendel, "Cultural Memory," *Reading Genesis: Ten Methods* (New York/Cambridge: Cambridge University Press, 2010)

28–46. Hendel builds upon the work of Jan Assman, *Moses The Egyptian: The Memory of Egypt in Western Monotheism* (Cambridge, MA: Harvard University Press, 1997) 8–9.

36. On the book of Samuel as a "remembered" past more generally, see Gilmour, *Representing the Past*, 31–3.

37. Blenkinsopp (*A History of Prophecy in Israel*, 52) notes these different typologies as well, though my ensuing discussion will highlight issues that he and others have not adequately addressed.

38. See chapter 2 of the present study for a discussion.

39. On Samuel as a symbol of the pre-monarchic priesthood, see Baruch Halpern, "The Uneasy Compromise: Israel Between League and Monarchy," *Traditions in Transformation: Turning Points in Biblical Faith* (ed. Baruch Halpern and Jon D. Levenson; Winona Lake: Eisenbrauns, 1981) 77.

40. Van der Toorn's brief comment that Samuel was a pre-monarchic "chief" like Gideon/Jerubbaal (*Family Religion*, 266) is insufficient in defining the pre-Deuteronomistic connection—or lack thereof—between these two characters, as will become clear in chapter 4 of the present study.

41. Brian Peckham, "Writing and Editing," *Fortunate The Eyes That See: Essays in Honor of David Noel Freedman in Celebration of His Seventieth Birthday* (ed. Astrid B. Beck et al.; Grand Rapids: Eerdmans, 1995) 364–83.

42. Here I refer to the proposed Prophetic Record as a redactional antecedent to the Deuteronomists' own work. The diverse views regarding this source have been discussed most extensively by Hutton, *Transjordanian Palimpsest*, 113–31, 152–6. The prophets highlighted in this source document often carry priestly–cultic duties or characteristics, and contrast the voices of the (roughly contemporary) 8th century prophets who sharply criticize the nation's cultic traditions. The discussion in chapter 2 of the present study will more clearly identify the disjunction as it relates to Samuel's place within the Prophetic Record, and will advance a proposal as to how the Deuteronomists rectified the problem.

43. On 1 Samuel 19:18–24, see Christophe Nihan, "Saul Among the Prophets (1 Sam 10:10–12 and 19:18–24): The Reworking of Saul's Figure in the Context of the Debate on 'Charismatic Prophecy' in the Persian Era," *Saul in Story and Tradition* (ed. Carl S. Erlich and Marsha C. White, FAT; Tubingen: Mohr Siebeck, 2006) 101–14. Nihan considers the passage as a reflection of Second Temple period resistance to ecstatic prophecy, though his observations regarding inner-Israelite divisions on prophetic phenomenology may also relate to earlier contexts; see chapter 2 of this study. On 1 Samuel 28, see Esther Hamori, "The Prophet and the Necromancer: Women's Divination for Kings," forthcoming in *JBL*.

CHAPTER I

1. The theory of a Deuteronomistic History was first proposed by Martin Noth, *Uberlieferungsgeschichtliche Studien* (Tübingen: JCM Mohr, 1957 [2nd ed.; original 1943]). For a full overview of scholarship on the Deuteronomistic History, see Mark Leuchter and Klaus-Peter Adam, "Introduction," *Soundings in Kings: Perspectives and Methods in Contemporary Scholarship* (ed. Mark Leuchter and Klaus-Peter Adam; Minneapolis: Fortress Press, 2010) 1–11.
2. Moshe Weinfeld's important proposals in this area helped to set the agenda for many scholars. See especially the introductory discussion in his *Deuteronomy 1–11* (AB; New York: Doubleday, 1991). His more extensive study, *Deuteronomy and the Deuteronomic School* (Oxford: Clarendon, 1972), remains a vital resource. In both works, he notes the connection between Deuteronomy and the northern prophetic tradition, but argues that the Deuteronomists were sage-scribes of the royal court (*Deuteronomy 1–11*, 45–50, 55–7, 65; *Deuteronomic School*, 177–8). An alternative proposal regarding the Deuteronomistic movement is that of Patricia Dutcher-Walls, "The Social Location of the Deuteronomists: a Sociological Study of Factional Politics in Late Pre-Exilic Judah," *JSOT* 52 (1991) 77–94, who views the Deuteronomists as a coalition drawing from a diverse social spectrum.
3. Hans Barstad, "The Understanding of the Prophets in Deuteronomy," *SJOT* 8 (1994) 236–51; Barstad sees the Deuteronomistic History beyond the book of Joshua as generally unfavorable to prophets.
4. Kratz, *Narrative Books*, 158–209.
5. Brian Peckham, *History and Prophecy: The Development of Late Judean Literary Traditions* (New York: Doubleday, 1993) 518–655.
6. Noll's "Deuteronomistic History or Deuteronomistic Debate?," in pre-published form, was one such paper (presented at the 2005 annual meeting).
7. For an overview of the major theories, see Thomas Römer, *The So-Called Deuteronomistic History* (London: T & T Clark, 2005) 21–43. See also Person's overview and proposal in his *The Deuteronomistic History and the Book of Chronicles*, 2–13.
8. Cross, *Canaanite Myth*, 274–89. See also the discussion by Richard D. Nelson, "The Double Redaction of the Deuteronomistic History: The Case Is Still Compelling" *JSOT* 293 (2005) 319–37; Richard Elliott Friedman, "From Egypt to Egypt: Dtr1 and Dtr2," *Traditions in Transformation*, 167–92. More recently, Römer has proposed a late 7th century BCE origin to the Deuteronomistic History subsequently expanded in the exilic

and Persian periods (*The So-Called Deuteronomistic History*, 43). See also Person, *The Deuteronomistic History and the Book of Chronicles*, for an in-depth discussion of an exilic/Persian period historiographic endeavor taking up pre-exilic sources.

9. On the Prophetic Record, see Hutton, *Transjordanian Palimpsest*, 152–6; McCarter, *I Samuel*, 18–23; Campbell, *Of Prophets and Kings*, passim. On a Hezekian-era historiography, see Baruch Halpern and David S. Vanderhooft, "The Editions of Kings in the 7th and 6th Centuries BCE," *HUCA* 62 (1991) 179–244; Helga Weippert, "Die deuteronomistischen Beurteilungen der Könige von Israel und Juda und das Problem der Redaktion der Königsbücher," *Bib* 53 (1972) 301–39. On an "Ephraimite" historiography, see Alexander Rofé, "Ephraimite versus Deuteronomistic History," *Reconsidering Israel and Judah: Recent Studies on the Deuteronomistic History* (ed. Gary N. Knoppers and J. Gordon McGonville; Winona Lake: Eisenbrauns, 2000) 462–74.

10. On Deuteronomy's reliance upon the Assyrian literature of the early–mid 7th century BCE, see Weinfeld, *Deuteronomy and the Deuteronomic School*, 91–100; Bernard M. Levinson, *Deuteronomy and the Hermeneutics of Legal Innovation* (New York/Oxford: Oxford University Press, 1997) 122–3, 134, 145, 147; Eckhart Otto, "Das Deuteronomium als archimedischer Punkt der Pentateuchkritik: Auf dem weg zu einer Neubergrundung der de Wettes'schen Hypothese," *Deuteronomy and Deuteronomic Literature* (Fs. C. H. W. Brekelmans, ed. M. Vervenne and J. Lust, BETL; Leuven: Leuven University Press, 1997) 321–39.

11. See, e.g., Friedman, "From Egypt to Egypt," 173–5.

12. Geoghegan, *The Time, Place and Purpose of the Deuteronomistic History*, 120–32.

13. For a major portion of this unit as characterizing Judahite religion, see Brettler, *The Creation of History*, 121. However, against Brettler's view that this was dislodged from a diatribe regarding Judah's own exile in 587 BCE, it seems just as likely that a writer used the fallen northern kingdom as a didactic vehicle to critique the practices of his contemporaneous late pre-exilic Judahite audience.

14. Bernard M. Levinson, "The Reconceptualization of Kingship in Deuteronomy and the Deuteronomistic History's Transformation of Torah," *VT* 51 (2001) 526–7. Levinson's suggestion that Deuteronomy must necessarily antedate the Josianic-era Deuteronomistic portrayal of kingship (p. 527) is a change from his earlier position that Deuteronomy was produced by Josiah's scribes (*Deuteronomy*, 9–10), though it still allows for Josiah to

theoretically have followed an older law code in carrying out his centralization program. See also Gary N. Knoppers, "Rethinking the Relationship Between Deuteronomy and the Deuteronomistic History: The Case of Kings," *CBQ* 63 (2001) 397–412; Gary N. Knoppers, *Two Nations Under God: The Deuteronomistic History of Solomon and the Dual Monarchies* (2 vols., HSM; Atlanta: Scholars, 1994) 1:134 and *passim*.

15. Levinson, "Reconceptualization," 527.
16. Marvin A. Sweeney, *King Josiah of Judah: The Lost Messiah of Israel* (New York/Oxford: Oxford University Press, 2001).
17. Sweeney, *King Josiah*, 160–2, 168–9.
18. Levinson, "Reconceptualization," 528–9. Levinson further engages the work of Udo Rüterswörden (*Von der politischen Gemeinschaft zur Gemeinde: Studien zu Dt 16,18–18,22* [BBB; Frankfurt: Athenaum, 1987] 94–111), wherein Rüterswörden argues for the law of the king as exilic and theoretical, whereas the earlier pre-exilic material was meant to be enforced and thus consistent with a monarchic-sponsored origin. Levinson criticizes Rüterswörden's view due to his position that the entirety of Deuteronomy was geared to be utopian ("Reconceptualization," 533–4). I am generally in agreement with Levinson's view, as I consider the law of the king to be pre-exilic as well. However, I will argue below that "utopian" is not an entirely fitting description of Deuteronomy's intended purpose.
19. Much of this view follows the assumption that literacy could only flourish in a multi-tiered state with a centralized urban administration, a position argued by David W. Jamieson-Drake, *Scribes and Schools in Monarchic Judah: A Socio-Archaeological Approach* (JSOTSup; Sheffield: Sheffield Academic Press, 1991). Though Jamieson-Drake is not mistaken in his conclusions regarding the type of conditions in a centralized state that lead to scribal resources, subsequent models of state formation and research into literacy and scribal practices require that the theory be adjusted and made significantly more flexible. For a consideration of alternatives that Jamieson-Drake did not address, see Leuchter, "Eisodus as Exodus," 324–7.
20. On priestly literacy, see Carr, *Tablet of the Heart*, 116–21. For recent discussions of Levites in the production of Deuteronomy, see William M. Schniedewind, *How the Bible Became a Book: The Textualization of Ancient Israel* (New York/Cambridge: Cambridge University Press, 2004) 110–14; Karel van der Toorn, *Scribal Culture and the Making of the Hebrew Bible* (Cambridge, MA: Harvard University Press, 2007) 51–108.
21. See Ryan Byrne, "The Refuge of Scribalism in Iron I Palestine," *BASOR* 345 (2007) 22–3, for the prospect of scribes recruited by retainers for

purposes of power consolidation or affirmation. See also the monograph-length study by Seth Sanders, *The Invention of Hebrew* (Urbana: University of Illinois Press, 2009), who discusses the standardization of pre-state scribal technologies and traditions via the foundation of the Israelite monarchic state(s). These studies point to the existence of different scribal–literary resources and outlets that antedate the establishment of the Israelite royal courts. Early and powerful priestly families in Israel would certainly have employed scribes for such purposes in advance of the rise of a monarchic state and assimilated them into the infrastructure of the major sanctuaries they helmed. Textuality, especially deployed for ritual or apotropaic purposes (see, e.g., Num 5), would have been part of the priestly education that Levites maintained even after the rise of the monarchy in the north.

22. J. R. Lundbom, "The Inclusio and Other Framing Devices in Deuteronomy i–xviii," *VT* 46 (1996) 314–15 (though I disagree with Lundbom's conclusion that Deuteronomy's contents originated as northern prophetic preaching); Mark Leuchter, *The Polemics of Exile in Jeremiah 26–45* (New York/Cambridge: Cambridge University Press, 2008) 105–7 and *passim*; see also Oded Lipschits, *The Fall and Rise of Jerusalem* (Winona Lake: Eisenbrauns, 2005) 84–5, for the close association between Jeremiah and these scribes. On the lineage roots of the Shaphanide scribal circle and their origins beginning in the Hezekian period (a time when northern refugees had begun to settle in Judah), see J. Andrew Dearman, "My Servants the Scribes: Composition and Context in Jeremiah 36," *JBL* 109 (1990) 418–20.

23. See the discussion by Jeffrey C. Geoghegan, *The Time, Place and Purpose of the Deuteronomistic History: The Evidence of "Until This Day"* (BJS; Providence: Brown University Press, 2006), 139–40, 149.

24. The assaultive nature of Josiah's centralization policies is discussed by Baruch Halpern, "Late Israelite Astronomies and the Early Greeks," *Symbiosis, Symbolism, and the Power of the Past* (ed. W. G. Dever and S. Gitin; Winona Lake: Eisenbrauns, 2003) 334–45.

25. Lauren A. S. Monroe, *Josiah's Reform and the Dynamics of Defilement* (New York/Oxford: Oxford University Press, 2010).

26. Monroe, *Dynamics of Defilement*, 23–43, 132.

27. Ibid. 77–119. Monroe accepts the arguments championed by Israel Knohl that the Holiness School was active already in the 8th–7th centuries BCE (*The Sanctuary of Silence: The Priestly Torah and the Holiness School* [Minneapolis: Fortress Press, 1995] 209). I agree that the Holiness School originated in the late 8th century BCE, though the evidence for

the mature form of the Holiness Code itself ("H"; Leviticus 17–26) suggests its formation in the exilic period or, possibly, later. See Bernard M. Levinson, "The Manumission of Hermeneutics: The Slave Laws of the Pentateuch as a Challenge to Contemporary Pentateuchal Theory," *Congress Volume 2004* (ed. Andre Lemaire, VTSup; Leiden: Brill, 2006) 305–22; Jeffrey R. Stackert, *Rewriting the Torah: Literary Revision in Deuteronomy and the Holiness Legislation* (FAT; Tubingen: Mohr Siebeck, 2007) 17–18; Christophe Nihan, "The Holiness Code Between D and P: Some Comments on the Function and Significance of Leviticus 17–26 in the Composition of the Torah," *Deuteronomium Zwischen Pentateuch und deuteronomischen Geschichtewerk* (ed. Eckart Otto and Reinhard Achenbach, FRLANT; Göttingen: Vandenhoeck and Ruprecht, 2004) 82–98. In my view, H draws from extant pre-exilic Holiness School thought and legal traditions, but was orchestrated by later hands.
28. Monroe, *Dynamics of Defilement*, 136–7.
29. Ibid. 133–6.
30. I do not, of course, deny that extensive reworking of Deuteronomy in the exilic or even post-exilic period took place. I suggest here only that a substantial amount of material approaching the mature form of Deuteronomy (especially chapters 5–28, though quite possibly other passages as well) were part of an original pre-exilic corpus.
31. Van der Toorn, *Scribal Culture*, 154.
32. Juha Pakkala, "The Date of the Oldest Edition of Deuteronomy," *ZAW* 121 (2009) 388–401.
33. This may account for the alternate sequence of events preserved in Chronicles, where Josiah's reform begins in 627 BCE and the law book is subsequently "found" in the temple. Details from the book of Jeremiah support this proposed sequence of events. The oracles many scholars identify as the earliest in Jeremiah's career—the early stratum of Jeremiah 30–31—are devoid of Deuteronomistic terminology or ideas beyond an advocacy of centralization in Jerusalem. Jeremiah 2–4, on the other hand, are also regarded as deriving from a Josianic background, but repeatedly allude to the laws of Deuteronomy. If the superscription to the book of Jeremiah carries any historical weight, then the initial version of Jeremiah 30–1 may derive from an early Josianic phase of Jeremiah's career, with Jeremiah 2–4 subsequently composed and delivered following the composition of Deuteronomy. On the Josianic provenance of these oracles, see Sweeney, *King Josiah*, 215–33 (though I must part ways at this point with Sweeney's reading of Jer 30–1

as pro-Deuteronomistic); Norbert Lohfink, "Der jungende Jeremia als Propagandist und Poet: zum Grundstock von Jer 30–31," *Le Livre de Jeremie: Le prophete et son milieu* (ed. P. M. Bogaert, BETL; Leuven: Peeters, 1997 [original, 1981]) 351–68; Ulrich Shroter, "Jeremias Botschaft fur die Nordreich: zu N. Lohfinks Uberlegungen zum Grundbestand von Jeremia xxx–xxxi," *VT* 35 (1985) 312–29.

34. On the royal-administrative tenor of these terms, see Moshe Weinfeld, "Judge and Officer in Ancient Israel," *IOS* 7 (1977) 65–88.

35. Norbert Lohfink argued for an exilic provenance to this unit, viewing it as a utopian image of leadership. See his essay "Die Sicherung der Wirksamkeit des Gotteswortes durch das Prinzip das Schriftlichkeit der Tora und das Prinzip der Gewaltenteilung nach der Ämtergesetzen des Buches Deuteronomium (Dt 16,18–18,22)" *Studien zum Deuteronomium und zur deuteronomistichen Literatur*, vol. 1 (SBAB; Stuttgart: Katholisches Bibelwerk, 1990) 305–23. The rhetorical effect of the unit as an ideological negotiation between royal and non-royal leadership, however, suggests otherwise.

36. Weinfeld, *Deuteronomy and the Deuteronomic School*, 91–100, 177–8.

37. For the use of this common motif, see Thomas C. Römer, "Transformations in Deuteronomistic and Biblical Historiographies: On "Book-Finding" and Other Literary Strategies," *ZAW* 109 (1997) 1–11.

38. Geoghegan noted this especially with regard to the "until this day" formulae, routinely attached as they are to episodes dealing with priesthood and the cult (*The Time, Place and Purpose of the Deuteronomistic History, passim*). This does not mean that all Levites stood in league with the Deuteronomistic tradition. Those who did appear to have been among a social elite and part of a royal and temple establishment (see below re: Jer 36), whereas others in the rural sector were burdened by socio-economic limitations as suggested by their categorization with the poor and disadvantaged within Deuteronomy.

39. Geoghegan, *The Time, Place and Purpose of the Deuteronomistic History*, 158–64. In support of Geohegan's proposed dating, one should note that most of the post-Josianic kings (Jehoahaz, Jehoiakim, and Jehoiachin) are condemned for following "all that [their] fathers had done," but Zedekiah is condemned for following "all that Jehoiakim had done" (2 Kgs 24:19). Jehoiakim's reign emerges as pivotal in the shift in historical perspective from the exilic Deuteronomists' point of view, and one may imagine that the creation of an ideology and accompanying historiography ignored by this king would factor into this perspective.

40. Geoghegan, *The Time, Place and Purpose of the Deuteronomistic History*, 138–40.
41. I have previously discussed the background to the production of this literary unit and its pre-exilic provenance. See Mark Leuchter, "The Sociolinguistic and Rhetorical Implications of the Source Citations in Kings," *Soundings in Kings*, 119–34.
42. See further Kratz, *Narrative Books*, 187–92.
43. In addition to the strategic consistency in the use of the phrase "until this day" found in Deuteronomy–Kings as highlighted by Geoghegan (*The Time, Place, and Purpose of the Deuteronomistic History, passim*), one thinks of the language of Josh 8:30–5, or the fronting of an early form of Judges 17–18 with Judges 17:1–6 to turn a pro-Jeroboam narrative into a critique of the northern monarchic institutions. On Judges 17:1–6 as a Deuteronomistic addition to an earlier pro-Jeroboam narrative, see Mark Leuchter, "Now There Was a [Certain] Man: Compositional Chronology in Judges–1 Samuel," *CBQ* 69 (2007) 436–7. The process of "looking ahead" in Joshua and Judges may actually be the result of a redactional "working back" from material in Samuel–Kings, a position espoused in a different way by Ernst Würthwein, "Erwagungen zum sog. deuteronomistischen Geschichtswerk: Eine Skizze," *Studien Zum Deuteronomistischen Geschichteswerk* (BZAW; Berlin: De Gruyter, 1994) 1–11.

CHAPTER 2

1. See, e.g., Gilmour, *Representing the Past*, 49; Antti Laato, "The Levitical Genealogies in 1 Chronicles 5–6 and the Formation of Levitical Ideology in Post-Exilic Judah," *JSOT* 62 (1994) 80, 82. These views, however, presuppose the concept of Levi as a tribe and (for Laato) *'ephrati* as a reference to "Ephraim" in 1 Samuel 1:1. I have elsewhere challenged this reading of *'ephrati* (Mark Leuchter, *Josiah's Reform and Jeremiah's Scroll: Historical Calamity and Prophetic Response* [Sheffield: Sheffield Phoenix Press, 2006] 22–3; Mark Leuchter, "Jeroboam the Ephratite," *JBL* 125 [2006] 60–1). Regardless of how one reads the term *'ephrati*, the real issue is the view of Levi as a tribe. Before the late pre-exilic period, to be a Levite was not a matter of "tribal" affiliation but occupying a social/sacral typology; see the ensuing discussion.
2. See especially Louis C. Jonker, "Reforming History: The Hermeneutical Significance of the Book of Chronicles," *VT* 57 (2007) 21–44.

3. Carol Meyers, "David As Temple Builder," *Ancient Israelite Religion: Essays in Honor of Frank Moore Cross* (ed. Patrick D. Miller et al.; Minneapolis: Fortress Press, 1987) 357–72.
4. On the interests of this document (if not its genuine contents), see Halpern, "The Uneasy Compromise," 81–4. See also Z. Ben-Barak, "The Mizpah Covenant: The Source of the Israelite Monarchic Covenant," *ZAW* 91 (1979) 30–43.
5. For a full discussion of the place of the reconstituted temple in Persian Yehud, see Peter R. Bedford, *Temple Restoration in Early Achaemenid Persia* (JSJSup; Leiden: Brill, 2001).
6. The construction of these Levite families is regarded by many to be a matter of incorporating non-Levites into the post-exilic Levitical ranks. This was first discussed by H. Gese ("Zur Geschichte der Kultsanger am zweiten Tempel," *Abraham unser Vater: Juden und Christen im Gespräche uber der Bibel* [Leiden: Brill, 1963] 222–34), who was followed by H. G. M. Williamson ("The Origins of the Twenty-Four Priestly Courses: A Study of 1 Chronicles xxiii–xxvii," *Studies in the Historical Books of the Old Testament* [ed. J. A. Emerton, VTSup; Leiden: Brill, 1979] 251–68) with some adjustments. See also Joachim Schaper, *Priester und Leviten im achämenidischen Juda* (FAT; Tübingen: Mohr Siebeck, 2000) 305.
7. For further discussion on these verses, see the conclusion to the present study.
8. Genealogies in general require such caution, as their textualization is largely informed by sociological or political agenda. For a recent discussion regarding the Chronicler's genealogical agenda, see Yigal Levin, "Who Was the Chronicler's Audience? A Hint From His Genealogies," *JBL* 122 (2003) 229–45. The topic has been most thoroughly addressed by Robert R. Wilson, *Genealogy and History in the Biblical World* (New Haven/London: Yale University Press, 1977), especially 27–36 (for the social function of alterations to genealogies).
9. The prophet, in this case, trumps other sacral typologies. Such is the underlying presumption of the Prophetic Record (McCarter, *I Samuel*, 18–23 and *passim*; Campbell, *Of Prophets and Kings*, 111–23; Hutton, *Transjordanian Palimpsest*, 152–6). Walter Dietrich's classic 1972 study identifies an exilic "prophetic" stratum (*Prophetie und Geschichte: Eine redaktionsgeschichtliche Untersuchung zum deuteronomistichen Geschichtswerk* [FRLANT; Gottingen: Vandenhoek & Ruprecht, 1972]), though as noted in chapter 1 of the present study, he has since adjusted his view in a number of significant respects (*The Early Monarchy in Israel*; "Prophetie im deuteronomistichen Geschichtswerk," *The Future of*

the Deuteronomistic History [ed. Thomas Romer, BETL; Leuven: Leuven University Press 2000] 47–65).

10. On the original connection of Exod 32:26–9 to the Massah–Meribah narrative in Exod 17:1b–7, see Joel S. Baden, "The Violent Origins of the Levites," *Levites and Priests in Biblical History and Tradition* (ed. Jeremy M. Hutton and Mark Leuchter; Atlanta: SBL, 2011) 103–16.

11. E.g., Cook, *Social Roots of Biblical Yahwism*, 57 (this is a point on which Cook and I disagree, though the remainder of his analysis of Levitical function is compelling); Laato, "Levitical Genealogies," 80, 82.

12. On endogamy and kinship networks, see Baruch Halpern, "Jerusalem and the Lineages in the Seventh Century BCE: Kinship and the Rise of Individual Moral Liability," *Law and Ideology in Monarchic Israel* (ed. Baruch Halpern and Deborah W. Hobson, JSOTSup; Sheffield: Sheffield Academic Press, 1991) 49–59. Kurt Mohlenbrink's extensive analysis of the Levitical genealogies remains the point of departure for understanding their function both socially and rhetorically ("Die levitischen Uberlieferungen des Alten Testaments," *ZAW* n.s. 11 [1934] 184–231).

13. For a concise discussion, see van der Toorn, *Family Religion*, 304. A folk etymology is provided in Gen 29:34, where Leah proclaims "now is the time when my husband will be attached (*yillaweh*) to me." The Pentateuchal Priestly writers know this meaning and use it to redefine the role of Levites in relation to the Aaronide priesthood in Num 18:2 (*wayillawu' eylekha*).

14. A. H. G. Gunneweg, *Leviten und Priester: Hauptlinien der Traditionsbildung und Geschichte des israelitisch-judischen Kultpersonals* (FRLANT; Gottingen: Vandenhoeck & Ruprecht, 1965) 38–44, 58.

15. Gösta W. Ahlström, *Royal Administration and National Religion in Ancient Palestine* (Leiden: Brill, 1982) 47–8; van der Toorn, *Family Religion*, 300–5.

16. Lawrence E. Stager, "The Archaeology of the Family in Ancient Israel," *BASOR* 260 (1985) 28.

17. Jeremy M. Hutton, "The Levitical Diaspora (I): A Sociological Comparison with Morocco's Ahansal," *Exploring the Longue Durée: Essays in Honor of Lawrence E. Stager* (ed. J. D. Schloen; Winona Lake: Eisenbrauns, 2009) 223–34; Jeremy M. Hutton, "All the King's Men," 121–51; Jeremy M. Hutton, "The Levitical Diaspora (II): Modern Perspectives on the Levitical Cities Lists (A Review of Opinions)," *Levites and Priests in Biblical History and Tradition*, 78–81.

18. Hutton, "Levitical Diaspora (I)."

19. Idem, "The Levitical Diaspora (II)," 78–81.

20. For pre-monarchic conditions that may have led to this outcome, see Meyers, "Kingship and Kinship," 181–3.

21. E.g., the position of Ahlström, *Royal Administration*, 44–8. Tribal status applied to the Levites is already assumed by the author of Exodus 2:1–10, who identifies Moses as born to a family of the Levite tribe. The date of this text is difficult to determine with any certainty, but the similarities to the Sargon birth legend (a product of the reign of Sargon II, ca. 720 BCE) suggests a late 8th–mid 7th century BCE period of composition.
22. I have retained here the antiquated language found in the JPS translation, as many scholars view this poem as quite ancient in origin, though debates continue as to assigning the poem a specific date. I prefer to see the poem as originated before the latter decades of the 8th century BCE, since the poet does not conceive of Levites in tribal terms (as does, for example, the author of Exod 2:1–10; see above).
23. While many scholars have followed Gunneweg that the "holy one" in this passage is a reference to Moses in the Massah-Meribah narrative of Exodus 17:1b-7 (*Leviten und Priester*, 38–9; Cross, *Canaanite Myth*, 197; van der Toorn, *Family Religion*, 303), Baden's recent argument that the Levite episode of Exodus 32:26–9 was once part of this narrative ("Violent Origins") opens the possibility that the "holy one" was a collective singular referring to all Levites. The plurals "*they* shall teach" and "*they* shall put incense" in Deuteronomy 33:10 suggest as much.
24. Stager, "Archaeology of the Family," 28.
25. Dever, *Who Were The Early Israelites*, 178–89. On the intertwining of the royal administration into cultic structures descending into peasant contexts, see Theodore J. Lewis, *Household and Family Religion in Antiquity* (ed. John Bodel and Saul M. Olyan; Malden, MA/Oxford: Blackwell, 2008) 72–7.
26. For recent studies of early poetry reflecting upon these cultural oppositions, see Mark Leuchter, "'Why Tarry the Wheels of His Chariot?' (Judg 5,28): Canaanite Chariots and Echoes of Egypt in the Song of Deborah," *Bib* 91 (2010) 256–68; Mark Leuchter, "Eisodus as Exodus: The Song of the Sea (Exod 15) Reconsidered," *Bib* 92 (2011) 321–46.
27. Cook, *Social Roots*, 231–4, 259–66.
28. Such is the reading suggested by Michael Fishbane, *Biblical Interpretation in Ancient Israel* (Oxford: Clarendon, 1985) 300, despite his comment regarding the wilderness as the "unsown steppe"; Theodore Hiebert, *The Yahwist's Landscape: Nature and Religion in Early Israel* (New York/Oxford: Oxford University Press, 1996) 9–12.
29. Smith, *The Origins of Biblical Monotheism*, 28.
30. See, for example, Fishbane, *Biblical Interpretation in Ancient Israel*, 300–4.

31. Determining a specific period for the origins of the Song of Moses is notoriously difficult, but a composition in the late 10th or early 9th century seems feasible; see Mark Leuchter, "Why is the Song of Moses in the Book of Deuteronomy?" *VT* 57 (2007) 314–17.
32. Weinfeld, *Deuteronomy and the Deuteronomic School*, 364–5; Paul Sanders, *The Provenance of Deuteronomy 32* (Leiden: Brill, 1996) 372–82 and *passim*; William L. Holladay, "Elusive Deuteronomists, Jeremiah and Proto-Deuteronomy," *CBQ* 66 (2004) 63–4.
33. Yair Hoffman notes this theme in Hosea with regard to the Exodus ("A North Israelite Typological Myth and a Judaen Historical Tradition: The Exodus in Hosea and Amos," *VT* 39 [1989] 170–7). That the Exodus is paired with the wilderness terminology in the aforementioned Hosean passage projects the same perspective on the wilderness tradition as the Exodus tradition, and its persistence in Jeremiah reinforces this purview.
34. Hutton, "Levitical Diaspora (II)," 80.
35. Smith, *Origins of Biblical Monotheism*, 27–9. This concept is reflected in the Priestly legislation regarding the scapegoat ritual in Leviticus 16: the goat carrying the corrupting influences of Israelite sin is sent out "to Azazel" in the wilderness.
36. Baden, "Violent Origins." See also Mark Leuchter, "The Fightin' Mushites," *VT* 62 (2012) 479–500.
37. I exclude from analysis 1 Samuel 2:1–10, a poem datable to the monarchic era but only secondarily worked into this narrative unit (McCarter, *I Samuel*, 75–6).
38. White, "The History of Saul's Rise," 287–8; Kratz, *Narrative Books*, 174; McCarter, *I Samuel*, 62–3, 65; Brettler, *The Creation of History in Ancient Israel*, 109; Dus, "Die Geburtslegende Samuels"; Blenkinsopp, *A History of Prophecy in Israel*, 52–3.
39. So also McCarter, *I Samuel*, 62–3; Dietrich, *The Early Monarchy*, 29–30.
40. Pace Dietrich, *The Early Monarchy*, 273, who states that "the story of Samuel's rise was told only with respect to his role in the foundation of the Israelite state and the enthronement of the first king."
41. With White, it seems reasonable to assume that Saulide writers shaped a narrative to ultimately legitimize Saul's aggression against the priesthood ("History of Saul's Rise," 292). However, this strikes me as a matter of adjustment to an extant tradition rather than wholesale original composition. Hutton discusses a similar scenario with another text related to Saul, i.e., the overwriting or reshaping of 1 Samuel 14:6–15 to pertain to Jonathan when it originally served as the conclusion to 1 Samuel 9:1–10:16 (*Transjordanian Palimpsest*, 357–61). If an original tradition could be

overwritten to replace Saul with Jonathan, an original tradition regarding Samuel could certainly have been similarly overwritten or retold to point ahead to Saul.

42. Of course, Moses' origins remain shrouded in mystery. Rudolph Smend noted that the only reliable details about the historical Moses are the Egyptian etymology of his name and the memory of his marriage into an important Midianite clan ("Mose als geschichtliche Gestalt," *HZ* 260 [1995] 15–16), though additional information has been proposed by Meindert Dijkstra, "Moses, the Man of God," *The Interpretation of Exodus: Essays in Honour of Cornelis Houtman* (ed. Riemer Roukema et al.; Leuven: Peeters, 2006) 17–36. Whatever the limitations we face in recovering a picture of the historical Moses, it appears to be the case that already by the first half of the 11th century, several priestly clans (the "Mushites," of which the Elides were one faction) drew sacral power from a claim of descent from Moses. See Leuchter, "Fightin' Mushites." For additional discussion regarding the Elide Mushite genealogical connection (and its relation to David's strategy of priestly politics), see Cross, *Canaanite Myth*, 195–215.

43. See Polzin, *Samuel and the Deuteronomist*, 23; Bodner, *1 Samuel*, 17.

44. On the intertwining structure, see Polzin, *Samuel and the Deuteronomist*, 39–40. For a discussion of the parent/child motif, see Bodner, *1 Samuel*, 30–4, 42. The surrogate parent/child relationship between Eli and Samuel is made clear in 1 Samuel 3:6, 16, where Eli refers to Samuel as his "son."

45. I translate here according to the LXX of 1 Samuel 2:27–8, which provides a clearer reading and declares plainly the charge given to Eli's ancestral house. The MT, by contrast, includes a minor scribal error (an addition of the letter *heh* at the outset of *nigloh nigleti*, creating *ha-nigloh nigleti*, "did I not indeed reveal myself...?" a rhetorical question) that does not match the tenor of the following verses. See further McCarter, *I Samuel*, 87.

46. Cross, *Canaanite Myth*, 196–8 (citing earlier arguments made by Wellhausen).

47. Hutton, "The Levitical Diaspora (I)," 229.

48. Van der Toorn, *Family Religion*, 194–8; Stager, "Archaeology of the Family," 20–2.

49. I use the term "Mosaic" to refer to language or ideas emulating Moses' individual sacral stature, whereas "Mushite" relates to matters concerned with claims to genealogical descent from Moses.

50. The remainder of the verse contains secondary clauses with Deuteronomistic language and reflects the hand of a later redactor, *pace* Menahem Haran, *Temples and Temple Service Ancient Israel* (Oxford: Clarendon,

1978) 98 n. 18. See Mark Leuchter, "Something Old, Something Older: Reconsidering 1 Samuel 2:27–36," *Perspectives on Hebrew Scriptures* (ed. Ehud Ben Zvi; Piscataway: Gorgias Press, 2006) 533–40.

51. Even the later Priestly recasting of the inauguration of the priesthood establishes a typological disconnection between Moses and Aaron, the latter of which receives vestments to initiate his office that are never given to Moses (Exod 39), and who takes on instructional authority regarding divine will that rivals Moses' own (Lev 10:11, 19–20). The views of McCarter (*I Samuel*, 91–3) and Marti J. Steussy (*Samuel and His God* [Columbia: University of South Carolina Press, 2010] 28–32) that 1 Samuel 2:35 pertains to Zadok and not Samuel overlook the possibility of a Deuteronomistic redactor augmenting an original tradition to account for later events in an exegetical manner (Leuchter, "Something Old, Something Older"). Steussy's additional hesitance to see Samuel carrying priestly characteristics is derived from her position that Samuel's ritual authority is due to his position as a "superprophet" extending into a typologically distinct priestly sphere (p. 32), but this is also problematic. Priests and prophets are not necessarily distinct types in early Israelite religion, and even in later periods the distinction between priestly and prophetic spheres of activity is not steadfast. See the discussion in chapter 3 of the present study.

52. Hutton, "The Levitical Diaspora," 227, 229.

53. This is elucidated further in the careful examination of George W. Savran, *Encountering the Divine: Theophany in Biblical Narrative* (London: Continuum, 2005) 41–6.

54. Pace Gnuse, "Reconsideration," 388–9.

55. See Wilson, *Prophecy and Society*, 172, for the role of prophecy as subsidiary to priestly status. We will explore this in greater depth in the next chapter of the present study.

56. Gnuse, "Reconsideration"; C. L. Seow, *Myth, Drama, and the Politics of David's Dance* (HSM 44; Atlanta: Scholars Press, 1989) 30–1.

57. Ibid., 11–54.

58. The LXX suggests the reading "YHWH called 'Samuel, Samuel!'" The MT reading seems equally plausible, however, and I have retained it here.

59. Gnuse, "Reconsideration," 383.

60. The *dabar* in prophetic texts is usually not connected to dream or vision reports, but constitutes the impulse empowering a coherent diatribe or critique (e.g., Amos 3–5; Mic 1; Hos 1:1–2; 4:1–19; Jer 7:1–2; 11:1; 25:1). The Jeremiah material is especially significant insofar as Jeremiah's visions (Jer 1:13–19; 24) are not classified under the rubric of the divine *dabar*.

The *locus classicus* for the distinction between dreams/visions and direct divine communication is Numbers 12:6–8 (which will be discussed below).

61. See here Gnuse's observations regarding the form-critical features of the narrative ("Reconsideration," 382–8). See also McCarter, *1 Samuel*, 98, who notes that the time of day conforms to ancient expectations regarding the reception of revelation.
62. Savran, *Encountering the Divine*, 46; Lyle Eslinger, *Kingship of God in Crisis* (Decatur: JSOT Press, 1985) 145–6.
63. On this last point, see Heller, *Power, Politics and Prophecy*, 67, though Heller does not specify that the ancestor in question is indeed Moses. On further connections between Moses and Samuel, see Rolf Rendtorff, "Samuel the Prophet: A Link Between Moses and the Kings," *The Quest for Context and Meaning: Studies in Biblical Intertextuality in Honor of James A. Sanders* (ed. Craig A. Evans and Shemaryahu Talmon; Leiden: Brill, 1997), 30–2, 34–6.
64. Cross, *Canaanite Myth*, 203 n. 35. The possible origin of this source is suggested below.
65. Seow, *Myth, Drama, and the Politics of David's Dance*, 31.
66. On incubation, see Thomas H. McAlpine, *Sleep, Divine and Human in the Old Testament* (JSOTSup; Sheffield: JSOT Press, 1987) 158–9. For 1 Samuel 3 as an incubation scene, see Steven von Wyrick, "El," *Eerdman's Dictionary of the Bible* (ed. David Noel Freedman; Grand Rapids: Eerdmans, 2000) 385; Blenkinsopp, *A History of Prophecy in Israel*, 52.
67. If, as Seow has argued, the Shiloh cult retained devotion to El, then such dream incubation may have been an inherited feature of the tradition at Shiloh at the time the Elides came to power over the site.
68. Leuchter, "Something Old, Something Older," 539–40. See also the comment by Heller, who notes that the oracle in 1 Samuel 2:27–36 lacks the expected reaction from Eli (*Power, Politics and Prophecy*, 46). 1 Samuel 3:16–18, however, *does* contain the expected reaction in response to Samuel relating the contents of his revelation to Eli, suggesting that in an earlier form, material in the anonymous prophet's oracle in the previous chapter was part of the episode involving Samuel and Eli. This and other points of contact (such as the *glh* terminology applied both to Samuel and the Moses in the anonymous prophet's oracle) suggest the original unity of the material.
69. Leuchter, "Eisodus as Exodus," 337–43.
70. On procreation as a sacral charge fostered among the pioneer families in early Israel, see Carol Meyers, *Discovering Eve: Ancient Israelite Women in Context* (New York; Oxford University Press, 1988) 95–121.

71. This same agrarian value system underlies Samuel's rebuke of kingship in 1 Samuel 8. Though the chapter's current form results from a Deuteronomistic scribal hand (Mark Leuchter, "A King Like All The Nations: The Composition of I Sam 8, 11–18," *ZAW* 117 [2005] 543–58), its sentiments preserve the agrarian, anti-monarchic ethic that characterized earliest Israelite rebukes of Canaanite-style monarchies. See the classic study by I. Mendelsohn, "Samuel's Denunciation of Kingship in Light of the Akkadian Documents from Ugarit," *BASOR* 143 (1956) 17–22. I would adjust my earlier view that Samuel's rebuke is entirely Deuteronomistic and suggest that while a Deuteronomist adjusted the particulars of the rebuke to align with Neo-Assyrian imperial experiences, the concept behind the rebuke itself is appropriate in the context of a Levitical–priestly critique of kingship.
72. Hutton, "The Levitical Diaspora (I)," 227. See also Leuchter, "Fightin' Mushites."

CHAPTER 3

1. See the concluding chapter of the present study for further discussion.
2. On the diversity of prophetic types and terms, see Blenkinsopp, *A History of Prophecy in Israel*, 27–9; Robert R. Wilson, *Prophecy and Society in Ancient Israel* (Minneapolis: Fortress Press, 1980) 136–41, 254–7. But see also Simon B. Parker, "Possession Trance and Prophecy in Pre-Exilic Israel," *VT* 28 (1978) 271–85 for ecstatic phenomenology including but also transcending prophetic categories.
3. On the problem of discerning between false oracles, spirits of falsehood, and "false prophets" themselves, see Esther Hamori, "The Spirit of Falsehood," *CBQ* 72 (2010) 15–30. On the broader issue of prophetic conflict rather than binary categories of true/false, see Burke O. Long, "Social Dimensions of Prophetic Conflict," *Semeia* 21 (1982) 31–43; Lester L. Grabbe, "Shaman, Preacher, or Spirit Medium? The Israelite Prophet in the Light of Anthropological Models," *Prophecy and Prophets in Ancient Israel* (ed. John Day, LHBOTS; London: T & T Clark, 2010) 117–32.
4. I have suggested this as a way of interpreting the underlying meaning of Deuteronomy 18:20–2, which lists criteria for evaluating prophecy that are exclusively retrospective: only after an evaluation of history can a prophet's words be judged "true," but this by definition precludes the directive to adhere to a contemporaneous prophecy (Deut 18:15). The process of evaluating whether or not a contemporaneous prophecy is binding is to compare it with the record of the words of earlier prophets

(Leuchter, *Josiah's Reform*, 46). Prophecy is thus a matter of ideological orthodoxy in Deuteronomy, suggesting that the matter was, for the authors of Deuteronomy, not a "live" issue, but a platform for advancing a theoretical social vision.

5. On Elijah as a legendary figure constructed for political purposes, see Marsha White, *The Elijah Legends and Jehu's Coup* (BJS; Atlanta: Scholars Press, 1997). Even if the Elijah legends were shaped with a specific goal in mind, they must draw from an extant folklore regarding him and other prophets like him. See Alexander Rofé, *The Prophetical Stories: The Narratives about the Prophets in the Hebrew Bible, their Literary Types and History* (Jerusalem: Magnes Press, 1988).

6. See Wilson, *Prophecy and Society*, 69–86, who discusses the distinction between "central" and "peripheral" prophets. Isaiah is clearly the former with regard to Judahite state religion, whereas Amos falls into the category of the latter during his mission to the north, an outsider kept at arm's length from the Beth El cult and dismissed from its precincts (Amos 7:10–17).

7. Fishbane notes, however, a polyvalent dimension to this passage that both denies the possibility of return and, at the same time, demands it (*Biblical Interpretation in Ancient Israel*, 310).

8. For a succinct discussion of this process, see van der Toorn, *Scribal Culture*, 252–9. The memory of the scribal canonization process is preserved by the rabbinic authors of Baba Bathra 14b–15a, where anonymous scribal groups are credited with "writing" Isaiah, Ezekiel, and the Book of the Twelve.

9. This was no doubt connected to Josiah's consolidation of power and the promotion of a Jerusalem-centered cultic policy which conflicted with hinterland tradition. On Deuteronomy 13 as preserving Josianic edicts silencing prophetic opposition, see van der Toorn, *Scribal Culture*, 154.

10. Blenkinsopp, *A History of Prophecy in Israel*, 3.

11. See Diana Edelman, "Of Priests and Prophets and Interpreting the Past: The Egyptian *Hm-Ntr* and *Hry-Hbt* and the Judahite *Nabi*'," *The Historian and the Bible: Essays in Honour of Lester L. Grabbe* (LHBOTS, ed. Philip R. Davies and Diana V. Edelman; London: T & T Clark, 2010) 103–11; Joachim Schaper, "Exilic and Post Exilic Prophecy and the Orality/Literacy Problem," *VT* 55 (2005) 334–5; Mark Leuchter, "The 'Prophets' and the 'Levites' in Josiah's Covenant Ceremony," *ZAW* 121 (2009) 31–47; van der Toorn, *Family Religion*, 306–15.

12. Debate ensues regarding the question of literary dependence of one passage upon the other. It seems to me more likely that each prophetic tradition is drawing from a common slogan or aphorism.

13. Cook, *Biblical Yahwism*, 231–66.
14. See my discussion of these verses in *Josiah's Reform*, 25–6. Wilson's view that Hosea's words here are a quotation of his detractors is informed by his view that Hosea's prophetic authority was rooted in ecstatic states of one form of another (*Prophecy and Society*, 226–7). I do not dispute Wilson's insights into the importance of ecstasy, but if one assumes that other forms of behavior or cognition could be understood as prophetic, then Hosea's words here take on a different valence and point to a distinction between prophetic types.
15. See especially Ahlström, *Royal Administration*, 48–51.
16. One may imagine, too, that this was sometimes effective. According to Amos 7:10–11, Amos' protests had done enough damage to move the priest Amaziah to contact the king with his concerns. See Blake Couey, "Amos vii 10–17 and Royal Attitudes Toward Prophecy in the Ancient Near East," *VT* 58 (2008) 310–13.
17. Such appears to be the influence of the "landed gentry" (*'am ha-'aretz*) who are able to intercede in Judah. Van der Toorn has suggested similar close involvement among the leading families in the north (*Family Religion*, 301 n. 55). The protests of Amos point to the elite of his day as beneficiaries of the state social and cultic policies. See further Walter L. Houston, "Was There a Social Crisis in the Eighth Century?" *In Search of Pre-Exilic Israel* (ed. J. Day, JSOTSup; London/New York: T & T Clark, 2004) 130–47 and Marvin L. Chaney, "Micah—Models Matter: Political Economy and Micah 6:9–15," *Ancient Israel: The Old Testament in its Social Context* (ed. Philip F. Esler; Minneapolis: Augsberg Fortress, 2006) 146–9 for an overview of socio-economic conditions favoring the elites to the injury of subsistence farmers in Amos' day.
18. Van der Toorn further notes the similarity between prophets and Levites in northern Israel during the monarchic period (*Family Religion*, 314–15).
19. Van der Toorn stops short of making this connection due to his proposal that the Levites were the official priests of the northern state cult and that the Exodus tradition was primarily the product of the northern state cult (*Family Religion*, 305, 312–13), but this is unlikely to have been the case. Though there are firm grounds for seeing the Exodus appropriated by the royal scribes of the northern state (Leuchter, "Fightin' Mushites," 496), the Levites' and prophets' connection to the Exodus tradition should rather be understood as a competing perspective to that constructed by the architects of the official northern state cult and drew from the pre-monarchic Exodus tradition.

20. For recent studies demonstrating these dynamics in ancient prophecy, see Martti Nissinen, "City as Lofty As Heaven: Arbela and Other Cities in Neo-Assyrian Prophecy," *Every City Shall Be Forsaken: Urbanism and Prophecy in Ancient Israel and the Near East* (ed. Lester L. Grabbe and Robert D. Haak; JSOTSup; Sheffield: Sheffield Academic Press, 2001) 172–209; Martti Nissinen, with Robert K. Rittner and C. L. Seow, (ed.), *Prophets and Prophecy in the Ancient Near East* (Atlanta: SBL, 2003) (for a collection of original sources in translation with helpful commentary); Martti Nissinen, (ed.) *Prophecy in its Ancient Near Eastern Context: Mesopotamian, Biblical and Arabian Perspectives* (Atlanta: SBL, 2000); Daniel E. Fleming, "Southern Mesopotamian Titles for Temple Personnel in the Mari Archives," *Inspired Speech: Prophecy in the Ancient Near East* (ed. John Kaltner and Louis Stulman, JSOTSup; London/New York: T and T Clark, 2004) 72–81; Steven W. Holloway, *Aššur is King! Aššur is King! Religion in the Exercise of Power in the Neo-Assyrian Empire* (Leiden: Brill, 2002); Matthjis De Jong, *Isaiah Among the Ancient near Eastern Prophets* (VTSup; Leiden: Brill, 2007) 171–86; Blake Couey, "Amos vii 10–17 and Royal Attitudes Towards Prophecy in the Ancient Near East," *VT* 58 (2008) 301–8.
21. Significant differences do emerge, however, with prophets such as Amos and those that receive attention in Samuel–Kings; see further below.
22. See the discussion of this verse in the previous chapter.
23. Leuchter, "Now There Was a [Certain] Man," 429–39.
24. See Leuchter, "Psalm xcix," 34.
25. Here we find an example of taphonomy as described by Miller, *Chieftains*, 104–5. On Shiloh as the central religious/administrative site in pre-monarchic Israel, see Halpern, "The Uneasy Compromise," 77.
26. For archaeological evidence regarding Judahite expansion in the 10th century, see Gunnar Lehmann, "The United Monarchy in the Countryside: Jerusalem, Judah and the Shephelah in the Tenth Century BCE," *Jerusalem in Bible and Archaeology: The First Temple Period* (ed. Andrew G. Vaughn and Ann E. Killebrew; Atlanta: SBL, 2003) 117–63. Even then, most scholars agree that population density would remain rather low until the mid to late 8th century BCE.
27. I have argued elsewhere, for example, that some evidence exists for a priestly "offshoot" of Shiloh stationed at or near Bethlehem/Ephratah, which accounts for the lore of devotion therein to the Shilonite Ark cult as attested in Psalm 132:6 (Leuchter, "Fightin' Mushites"), 487–9.
28. Richard D. Nelson, "The Double Redaction of the Deuteronomistic History: The Case is Still Compelling," *JSOT* 29.3 (2005) 325–6.

29. See, however, the discussion in chapter 1 of the present study regarding a social and historical background to the Deuteronomists' activity.
30. Though as discussed in the introduction to the present study, this is a matter of late redactional shaping of the accounts associated with the reign of these kings.
31. The Deuteronomists, of course, are following extant concepts regarding Shiloh and Jerusalem as discussed in the previous chapter of the present study. But the royal connection to Joshua's leadership typology—rather than adherence to the traditional Davidic *mythos*—is a particularly Deuteronomistic innovation. See Monroe, *Dynamics of Defilement*, 136–7.
32. Phyllis Tribble, *Texts of Terror: A Literary-Feminist Reading of Biblical Narrative* (Minneapolis: Fortress Press, 1984) 65–91.
33. See especially J. Cheryl Exum, "The Center Cannot Hold: Thematic and Textual Instabilities in Judges," *CBQ* 52 (1990) 410–31.
34. On the harvest festival at Shiloh, see Ackerman, *Warrior, Dancer*, 254–76.
35. Robert H. O'Connell, *The Rhetoric of the Book of Judges* (VTSup; Leiden: Brill, 1996) 323; Donald G. Schley, *Shiloh: A Biblical City in Tradition and History* (JSOTSup; Sheffield: Sheffield Academic Press, 1989) 136.
36. Schley, *Shiloh*, 131–2, 136.
37. On the pre-Israelite cult at Shiloh, see Benjamin C. Ollenburger, *Zion, City of the Great King: A Theological Symbol of the Jerusalem Cult* (JSOTSup; Sheffield: Sheffield Academic Press, 1987) 38–43.
38. Erik Eynikel ("Judges 19–21, An Appendix: Rape, Murder, War and Abduction," *Communio Viatorum* 47 [2005] 100–15) comes to a similar conclusion, noting that kingship in and of itself still required YHWH's *torah* (conveyed through prophecy, as I have discussed above): "When God and his Thora [sic], as in Judges 19–21 are (almost) absent, every man (or every group) does what is right in his own eyes" (pg. 115), to tragic effect.
39. The words of the anonymous prophet were once part of an oracle attributed to Samuel himself (Leuchter, "Something Old, Something Older"). A later redactor has separated these words from Samuel, but it is notable that they are placed in a chapter so strongly connected to Samuel's own sacral growth.
40. The LXX parallel omits the final "at Shiloh through the word of YHWH," suggesting that the pre-Deuteronomistic form of the tradition concluded simply with the statement that "YHWH revealed himself to Samuel." The LXX does include other details that are not included in the MT, however; see McCarter, *I Samuel*, 97.

41. McCarter suggests that the MT version's lack of the emphasis contrasting Samuel to the Elides is the result of scribal error (*I Samuel*, 97). However, this may have been a deliberate move by an early editor which emphasizes the place of Shiloh in the Deuteronomistic History. The LXX may thus reflect an earlier version of the tradition before its alignment with Joshua–Judges.
42. It is noteworthy, too, that the Jeremiah tradition presents a similar characterization of the prophet, insofar as Jeremiah commissions a non-priest/non-prophet—Baruch—to be the trustee of his legacy (Jer 45).
43. See below for further comment. On the pre-Deuteronomistic layer of the chapter, see Hutton, *Transjordanian Palimpsest*, 311 n. 57.
44. This supports the theory of a Prophetic Record as a major stop along the way toward the canonical shape of Samuel–Kings.
45. For a thorough analysis of Jeremiah's engagement of 8th-century prophecy, see H. Lalleman-de Winkel, *Jeremiah in Prophetic Tradition: An Examination of the Book of Jeremiah in the Light of Israel's Prophetic Traditions* (Leuven: Peeters, 2000).
46. On the emendation from the MT "the voice of YHWH's words," see McCarter, *I Samuel*, 260.
47. On the emendation of the Hebrew term to *haharamto*, see McCarter, *1 Samuel*, 261.
48. See the comments by Bodner, *1 Samuel*, 156. For a full study of the *herem*, see Philip D. Stern, *The Biblical Herem: A Window On Israel's Religious Experience* (BJS; Atlanta: Scholars Press, 1991). On its function in state formation, see Monroe, *Dynamics of Defilement*, 48–56. A mythological background to the *herem* that also carries sacrificial overtones is discussed by Smith, *Origins of Biblical Monotheism*, 162.
49. Hutton, *Transjordanian Palimpsest*, 311; McCarter, *I Samuel*, 20; Campbell, *Of Prophets and Kings*, 68–9; Dietrich, *The Early Monarchy*, 246.
50. On the *teraphim* as iconographic representations of the ancestors, see van der Toorn, *Family Religion*, 219–25.
51. This deference to prophecy, it may be argued, may also be part of the chapter's origins with the Prophetic Record. Yet it seems to me that the additional lexical features of these verses are rather close to Deuteronomistic texts that outlaw competing forms of divination very similar to this in 1 Samuel 15:22–3 (e.g., Deut 18:9–14; 2 Kgs 23:24) and show knowledge of the anti-sacrifice theme running through the prophetic texts surveyed below. These verses may thus be viewed as Deuteronomistic, but as advancing concepts already inherent to the source the Deuteronomists received.

52. The Jeremianic verses are of course beyond the Deuteronomistic History, but as virtually all scholars recognize, the book of Jeremiah stands within the Deuteronomistic tradition and constitutes another "chapter" in the development of Deuteronomistic thought. See Leuchter, *Polemics of Exile*, 9–13.
53. Jonathan S. Greer, "A Marzeah and a Mizraq: A Prophet's Mêlée with Religious Diversity in Amos 6.4–7," *JSOT* 322 (2007) 243–62; Hans M. Barstad, *The Religious Polemics of Amos* (Leiden: Brill, 1984) 127–42.
54. Compare this to Jeremiah 34:8–22, where Jeremiah harangues Zedekiah and the elite of Jerusalem for a ritual decree of amnesty for debt-slaves followed by a reclaiming of those same slaves by their former owners.
55. On idol production in the ancient near east, see Thorkild Jacobsen, "The Graven Image," *Ancient Israelite Religion*, 15–29. Jeremiah 10:1–16 demonstrates the intimate familiarity of Israelites with these same rites of production.
56. The rhetorical force of this language is certainly amplified by Hosea's own priestly heritage. See Cook, *Social Roots*, 231–66.
57. Nadav Na'aman has criticized the view that northern refugees fled to Judah in the late 8th century; see his essay "When and How Did Jerusalem Become a Great City? The Rise of Jerusalem as Judah's Premier City in the Eighth–Seventh Centuries BCE," *BASOR* 347 (2007) 21–48. However, the majority of scholars accept the likelihood that northern refugees fled southward. See Schniedwind, *How The Bible Became A Book*, 66–90; Israel Finkelstein and Neil Asher Silberman, "Temple and Dynasty: Hezekiah, The Remaking of Judah, and the Rise of the Pan-Israelite Ideology," *JSOT* 30.3 (2006) 259–85; Geoghegan, *The Time, Place and Purpose of the Deuteronomistic History*, 149–50; Pamela Barmash, "At The Nexus of History and Memory: The Ten Lost Tribes," *AJS Review* 29 (2005) 207–36; Gary A. Rendsburg and William M. Schniedwind, "The Siloam Tunnel Inscription: Historical and Linguistic Perspectives," *IEJ* 60 (2010) 188–203.
58. Pace Nadav Na'aman, "The Israelite–Judahite Struggle for the Patrimony of Ancient Israel," *Bib* 91 (2010) 20, who suggests that Josiah's expedition to Bethel was the vehicle for the discovery and transmission of the writings of these prophets into the hands of Jerusalemite scribes.
59. Similar socio-economic circumstances in Judah in comparison to the conditions a generation earlier in the north, however, certainly facilitated the common shape of these prophetic critiques. See Houston, "Social Crisis."
60. The passages in Jeremiah 19 are somewhat veiled insofar as they refer only to the *tophet*, but this term is widely regarded as a type of apparatus

devoted to such sacrifice. For a detailed discussion, see Francesca Stavrakopoulou, *King Manasseh and Child Sacrifice: Biblical Distortions of Historical Realities* (BZAW; Berlin: De Gruyter, 2004) 152–3. See also her discussion of child sacrifice as a Yahwistic practice on pp. 179–206.

61. H. G. M. Williamson notes the difficulty in assigning a particular date to these verses, though he is inclined to view them as dating to before the Assyrian crisis of 701 BCE. See his *Isaiah 1–5* (ICC; London/New York: T & T Clark, 2006) 85.

62. For the positions of Sakkuth and Kaiwan in the Mesopotamian pantheon, see Marvin A. Sweeney, *The Twelve Prophets* (Berit Olam; Collegeville: Liturgical Press, 2000) 241. On the Assyrian control of Aramean territory during the first half of the 8th century and intermittent struggle until roughly 750, see John Barton, *Amos's Oracles Against the Nations* (Cambridge: Cambridge University Press, 1980) 30–1.

63. Stavrakopoulou, *King Manasseh and Child Sacrifice*, 148–79.

64. See Halpern, "Jerusalem and the Lineages," 91, for the rejection of certain older traditions as foreign. See also Halpern, "Brisker Pipes Than Poetry: The Development of Israelite Monotheism," *Judaic Perspectives on Ancient Israel* (ed. Jacob Neusner et al.; Philadelphia: Fortress Press, 1987) 92–7 for antecedents to this already at work earlier in the 8th century BCE.

65. See, among others, Cook, *Social Roots*, 234.

66. See the previous chapter under the section heading "The Agrarian Motif in Levitical Tradition"; Leuchter, "Eisodus as Exodus," 337–43.

67. Dever, *Who Were The Early Israelites?*, 198.

68. Ibid., 198.

69. On "chaos" see Bodner, *1 Samuel*, 115. On "nothingness," see David T. Tsumura, *The First Book of Samuel* (NICOT; Grand Rapids: Eerdmans, 2007) 329 n. 52. I do not share Tsumura's opinion, though, that "chaos" is beyond the interpretive pale; see immediately below.

70. McCarter, *1 Samuel*, 217.

71. This same concept is found in Jeremiah 44, where Jeremiah's Deuteronomistic admonitions are rejected by the Judahites who have fled to Egypt; they in turn are cut off from the covenant, their Israelite identity stripped by YHWH, and they revert to foreign (Egyptian) status. Not coincidentally, the first oracle against foreign nations following this episode (in the MT) is an oracle against Egypt. See Leuchter, *Polemics of Exile*, 134–6.

72. Tsumura, *The First Book of Samuel*, 329, ad. loc. n. 52.

73. Leuchter, "Eisodus as Exodus," 344–6.

74. Schloen, "Casus Belli," 35–8.

75. Louis H. Feldman notes that in Exodus 17:14, YHWH claims that he himself will destroy Amalek; in Deuteronomy, it is Israel that is charged with this responsibility (*Remember Amalek!: Vengeance, Zealotry and Group Destruction in the Bible according to Philo, Pseudo-Philo and Josephus* [Cincinatti: Hebrew Union College Press, 2004] 9).

76. One key term that suggests this was the intention is *ma'adannot*, "[bound] in chains," in 1 Samuel 15:32; from the root *'anad*, "bound," which here appears to have been metathesized. The other possible translation of this term, "in good spirits," seems highly unlikely given the circumstances. A similar type scene is found in 2 Kings 23:33 with the binding and capture of Jehoahaz by Necho, and in 2 Kings 25:7 with the binding and capture of Zedekiah by Nebuchadnezzar's forces. Saul's behavior thus appears to follow ancient convention. Connections are often drawn between Saul's actions and the charge to Joshua to retain spoils of war from Ai (Josh 8:2), but the parallel is not as strong. Joshua 8:2 specifies that the king of Ai was to be killed, and Joshua 8:17 makes clear that this charge was carried out.

77. When one factors into this meditation Monroe's observation that the *herem* is a foundational institution in state formation (*Dynamics of Defilement*, 48–56), the stakes are raised even higher in terms of establishing a tenable basis for a monarchic society.

78. See chapter 1 of the present study.

79. In Deuteronomy, these verses identify the ultimate authorities as the Levitical priests. Yet in broader context, this is not inconsistent with the idea of prophetic leadership, especially if Samuel is symbolic of the merging of these typologies.

80. On the prophet as sentinel, see Lena-Sofia Tiemeyer, "The Watchman Metaphor in Isaiah lvi–lxvi," *VT* 55 (2005) 378–400.

CHAPTER 4

1. David Jobling, *1 Samuel* (Berit Olam; Collegeville: Liturgical Press, 1998) 29–34; Edelman, *King Saul*, 37–8; Bodner, *1 Samuel*, 3, 49.

2. So also Edelman, *King Saul*, 38.

3. Deuteronomy itself bears the greatest testimony to the diverse applicability of the *šophet* role. It identifies a *šophet* as part of the central sanctuary and as distinct from the Levitical priests (Deut 17:9, 11), but it is clear that Levite priests have the final say on the transmission of law and covenantal standards (Deut 11; 27; 30:9–13). The demotion of both the monarch *and* elders to subordinates of the Levitical priests is

suggestive of the juridical role both traditionally held that the authors of Deuteronomy wished to curb; see Levinson, *Deuteronomy*, 125–6.
4. See Levinson, "Reconceptualization," 515–16.
5. For an overview of this dynamic, see Joshua Berman, *Created Equal: How The Bible Broke With Ancient Political Thought* (New York/Oxford: Oxford University Press, 2008) 18–49, 51–80.
6. See Simeon Chavel, "Oracular Novellae and Biblical Historiography: Through the Lens of Law and Narrative," *Clio* 39 (2009) 1–27.
7. Moses is, admittedly, not referred to as a *šophet* in this passage, but his function is identical to that of the *šophet* in Deuteronomy 17:9, 11, who secures a divine ruling in the face of a troubling case.
8. On the dramatic break from conventional ancient jurisprudence in these verses, see Levinson, *Deuteronomy*, 100–33.
9. As Levinson has discussed, Deuteronomy (7th–6th centuries) revises the Covenant Code (late 8th–mid 7th centuries), and the Holiness Code revises both ("Manumission of Hermeneutics").
10. I am indebted to Christophe Nihan for sharing his analysis of these verses with me in a pre-published version of his paper "How Samuel Became a 'Deuteronomistic' Book: 1 Samuel 8 and 12 and the Alignment of 1–2 Samuel with Deuteronomy," presented at the 2011 Annual Meeting of the Society of Biblical Literature.
11. So also Edelman, *King Saul*, 74–5.
12. Miller, *Chieftains*, 8–9.
13. See, e.g., Flanagan, "Chiefs in Israel." We shall return to this point below.
14. Halpern, "The Uneasy Compromise," 75–6 n. 54. See also Timothy M. Willis, "The Nature of Jephtah's Authority," *CBQ* 59 (1997) 43 n. 34.
15. On the scribal technique of "fronting," see Sarah Milstein, "Reworking Ancient Texts: Revision Through Introduction in Biblical and Mesopotamian Literature" (Ph.D. Diss., New York University, 2010).
16. The LXX reads "Samson" rather than "Samuel," but most commentators accept the MT reading as it stands.
17. Halpern similarly notes that Gideon decides to "don the cloth" in capitalizing on his successful conduct of battle ("The Uneasy Compromise," 76).
18. That a Deuteronomistic redactor shares language with Hosea in this regard is not surprising given the commonalities shared between Hosea and Deuteronomy (Weinfeld, *Deuteronomy 1–11*, 45–50).
19. The two do not seem to be the same item, since Gideon's *ephod* is a sort of totem or cultic fetish while Samuel's is a garment.

20. Halpern, "The Uneasy Compromise," 68.
21. Meyers, *Discovering Eve*, 95–121.
22. On the Gideon–Abimelekh narrative as an account of the ineffectual transition from chiefdom to monarchy, see Katie M. Heffelfinger, 'My Father is King': Chiefly Politics and the Rise and Fall of Abimelech," *JSOT* 33.3 (2009) 277–92.
23. So also H. G. M. Williamson, "Prophetesses in the Hebrew Bible," *Prophecy and Prophets in the Hebrew Bible* (ed. John Day; New York/London: T & T Clark, 2010) 68.
24. The antiquity of the poem in Judges 5 is almost unanimously accepted, with degrees of variation regarding its specific age or the stages of development it represents. For an overview of scholarship, see Leuchter, "Why Tarry the Wheels of His Chariot?," 256 n. 1.
25. Williamson, "Prophetesses," 67–8; Blenkinsopp, *A History of Prophecy*, 51.
26. Raymond de Hoop, "Judges 5 Reconsidered: Which Tribes? What Land? Whose Song?," *The Land of Israel in Bible, History and Theology* (ed. J. Van Ruiten and J. C. De Vos, VTSup; Leiden: Brill, 2009) 151–66. Ackerman takes the issue further by raising the possibility that Deborah herself does not correspond to an historical individual ("Why Is Miriam Also Among the Prophets?," 62).
27. See also Klaas Spronk, "Deborah, A Prophetess: The Meaning and Background of Judges 4:4–5," *The Elusive Prophet: The Prophet as a Historical Person, Literary Character, and Anonymous Artist* (ed. Johannes C. de Moor, VTSup; Leiden: Brill, 2001) 232–42.
28. Williamson has noted this parallel as well ("Prophetesses," 68; I am especially happy to refer the reader to the contents of n. 9 on that page).
29. So also Ackerman, *Warrior, Dancer*, 107; Williamson, "Prophetesses," 72. This also recalls Würthwein's proposal regarding a working back from Kings to the earlier books in the Deuteronomistic History ("Erwagungen zum sog. deuteronomistischen Geschichteswerk"), though in agreement with both Ackerman and Williamson, the passages noted here may have been simultaneously developed, with the Kings *source* material involving Huldah (Monroe, *Dynamics of Defilement* 59, though she points to the current shape of the oracle as originating in the Deuteronomists' work) as the motivating tradition leading to this overall redactional shaping.
30. See especially Spronk, "Deborah," 238, who suggests that the term *išah nebi'ah* was added to identify her brand of oracular authority as legitimate over against competing types.

31. So too the unique masculine parallel to this, the *'ish nabi'* affixed to the redactionally inserted anonymous prophet in Judges 6. See Williamson, "Prophetesses," 68; Spronk, "Deborah," 238.
32. Ackerman, *Warrior, Dancer*, 38.
33. Leuchter, "Why Tarry The Wheels of His Chariot?." Ackerman suggests that the term connects to Deborah's original cultic function (*Warrior, Dancer*, 108).
34. See the similar conclusion reached by Williamson, "Prophetesses," 69–73.
35. Max Weber, *The Theory of Social and Economic Organization* (New York: Free Press, 1947) 358.
36. Edelman, *King Saul*, 34.
37. *Pace* Wilson, *Prophecy and Society*, whose working assumption is that ecstasy is the basis for prophetic authority and thus Samuel must have been regarded as an ecstatic.
38. See Blenkinsopp, *A History of Prophecy in Israel*, 53, who comes to a similar conclusion.
39. Leuchter, *Josiah's Reform*, 24–5. See also Tiemeyer, "Watchman."
40. See, e.g., van der Toorn, *Family Religion*, 191. In an earlier study (*Josiah's Reform*, 29), I argued for reading *zuph/zopheh* as a prophetic typology, though following van der Toorn and others, *zuph* is presented here as a clan name. However, as I discuss in these pages and in chapter 2 of the present study, kinship networks can and do form around sacral institutions and behavior, and prophetic behavior can be a defining element of clan identity.
41. Van der Toorn, *Family Religion*, 309–10, 312.
42. See Edelman, *King Saul*, 38. Samson's case is unique, as the Samson narrative seems to be rooted in an early folkloristic tale rather than a legend regarding a warrior–savior with a political legacy. Nevertheless, the pre-monarchic temporal setting of this folkloristic tradition and the fact that it relates to violent conflict between an Israelite and the Philistines provided the redactors of the book of Judges with enough justification to include Samson into their work.
43. See the detailed analysis by Hutton, *Transjordanian Palimpsest*, 313–22. Edelman notes, though, that the closing verses of the preceding chapter anticipate the events of 1 Samuel 11 (*King Saul*, 59). In my view, this reflects the harmonizing redactional strategy of the Deuteronomists, since the event in 1 Samuel 10:17–27 otherwise conforms to pre-Deuteronomistic parallels in Joshua 7:14–18 and 1 Samuel 14:14–20 (following McCarter, *I Samuel*, 195–6).

44. *Pace* the argument of Beyerlin, who claimed that Saul's charisma is to be associated with his prophetic experience and his anointing by Samuel ("Das Konigscharisma bei Saul"). The distinction between 1 Samuel 11 and 9:1–10:16 points to different narrative purposes and appeals to different cultural institutions; taken on its own, 1 Samuel 11 is very much in the tradition of the judges who precede Saul.
45. Hutton, *Transjordanian Palimpsest*, 313–21. Edelman notes further resonances with the narratives from Judges in 1 Samuel 9:16 as well (*King Saul*, 48). Though Edelman sees this as an original part of the narrative, I would suggest that this is the result of a redactional addition, carrying a type of private message from YHWH that we encounter in 1 Samuel 16:1–3, 7, which derive from either a Deuteronomistic redaction or within the Prophetic Record (Hutton, *Transjordanian Palimpsest*, 251–2, 332–3; see similarly Blenkinsopp, *A History of Prophecy in Israel*, 53). In agreement with Edelman, the narrative *implies* that Samuel is the seer from the outset, but this does not negate Hutton's view that the actual name of Samuel was introduced by a later redactor. The narrative may have been intended to stop short of naming Samuel due to the extant association between Samuel's Levite support group and David. Sensing this, the later redactor filled in the blanks, so to speak.
46. On this definition, see Halpern, "Uneasy Compromise," 71–2.
47. Bodner, *1 Samuel*, 79.
48. Daniel E. Fleming, *Democracy's Ancient Ancestors: Mari and Early Collective Governance* (New York/Cambridge: Cambridge University Press, 2004); Daniel E. Fleming, "Mari and the Possibilities of Biblical Memory," *RA* 92 (1998) 41–78.
49. Lengthy genealogies embedded in narrative contexts serve emphatic purposes and highlight the importance of the figure in question. David A. Glatt-Gilad discusses this with regard to the narratives of Jeremiah ("The Personal Names in Jeremiah as a Source for the History of the Period," *Hebrew Studies* 41 [2000] 31–45), but the same can be said about the extended genealogies for Ezra (Ezra 7:1–5), for Samuel's father Elkanah (1 Sam 1:1) and, obviously, for Kish at the outset of the Saul tale.
50. The term is applied to Gideon (Judg 6:12) and Jephtah (Judg 11:1), both of whom attain chieftain status, as well as to David (1 Sam 16:18) and Jeroboam (1 Kgs 11:28), both of whom attain monarchic status derived from extant socio-political clout.
51. Siegfried Kreutzer, "Saul—Not Always—At War: A New Perspective on the Rise of Kingship in Israel," *Saul in Story and Tradition* (ed. Carl S. Ehrlich and Marsha C. White, FAT; Tübingen: Mohr Siebeck, 2006)

39–56. See also Israel Finkelstein, "The Last Labayu: King Saul and the Expansion of the First Northern Israelite Territorial Entity," *Essays on Ancient Israel in its Near Eastern Context: A Tribute to Nadav Na'aman* (ed. Yairah Amit et al.; Winona Lake: Eisenbrauns, 2006) 171–87, though Finkelstein conceives of Saul's rise as a local strongman against a later temporal context (10th century BCE) than the 11th-century setting accepted by most scholars.

52. Kreutzer, "Saul," 46–8.
53. Van der Toorn is correct to ascribe much influence to the religious developments emerging from Saul's proto-state and eventually woven into the theological fabric of Israel in successive periods (*Family Religion*, 266–86). The expanse of this proto-state would have been relatively limited and appears to correspond to the expanse of Samuel's own jurisdiction as a circuit-court judge in 1 Samuel 7; see Edelman, *King Saul*, 43–4. Nevertheless, this geographical dominion was sufficient to form the basis for incursions into adjacent areas and establishing a presence in local political and economic processes.
54. See the discussion in chapter 2 of the present study.
55. This, perhaps, accounts for the overlap/transition between Samuel and Saul as contesting leaders over the same population in 1 Samuel 8–12. Though Samuel brings the era of the judges to an end in 1 Samuel 7 and the monarchy begins properly in 1 Samuel 13, the intervening chapters and their ambiguities signify a period of struggle between both leadership types.
56. Miller, *Chieftains*, 8. See also Higginbotham, *Elite Emulation*, 132–42, for regional Egyptian control throughout the area.
57. Friedman, "From Egypt to Egypt." See also Garett Galvin, *Egypt as a Place of Refuge* (FAT; Tübingen: Mohr Siebeck, 2011).
58. See further Robert D. Miller, "When Pharaohs Ruled: On the Interpretation of Judges 5:2," *JTS* 59 (2008) 650–4.
59. Edelman, *King Saul*, 44–5.
60. Ibid., 27, 29.
61. Miller, *Chieftains*, 9.
62. Such was, as Stager notes, the norm that was successfully adopted and implemented by Solomon ("The Patrimonial Kingdom of Solomon") and which had long existed in west-Semitic environs. See J. David Schloen, *The House of the Father as Fact and Symbol: Patrimonialism in Ugarit and the Ancient Near East* (Winona Lake: Eisenbrauns, 2001). Parallels within the Saul narratives and Hittite texts suggest that Saul attempted to structure his administration upon well-founded Bronze

Age monarchic praxes, including expectations of patrimonial allegiance; see Ada Taggar-Cohen, "Political Loyalty in the Biblical Account of 1 Samuel xx–xxii in the light of Hittite Texts," *VT* 55 (2005) 253–4, 260–2, 265–8. Similar implications arise from the events in 1 Samuel 20, where Saul fully expects David to place the royal feast above his own clan obligations.

63. Taggar Cohen, "Political Loyalty," 265–8.
64. See Diana Edelman, "Did Saulide–Davidide Rivalry Resurface in Early Persian Yehud?," *The Land That I Will Show You: Essays on the History and Archaeology of the Ancient Near East in Honor of J. Maxwell Miller* (ed. J. Andrew Dearman and M. Patrick Graham, JSOTSup; Sheffield: Sheffield Academic Press, 2001) 77–83.
65. See Halpern, "Jerusalem and the Lineages," 21–49, for an overview of Hezekiah's actions and policies relating to Assyrian suzerainty.
66. See Brettler, *Creation of History*, 109–11; Edelman, *King Saul*, 19–24; Edelman, "Saulide–Davidic Rivalry"; Yaira Amit, "The Saul Polemic in the Persian Period," *Judah and the Judeans in the Persian Period* (ed. Oded Lipschits and Manfred Oeming; Winona Lake: Eisenbrauns, 2006) 647–61; Russell Hobson, "Jeremiah 41 and the Ammonite Alliance," *Journal of Hebrew Scriptures* 10 (2010) Article 7, esp. 14–15.
67. On Mizpah as an administrative center, see Lipschits, *The Fall and Rise of Jerusalem*, 87–9, 92, 95–7, 99–102.
68. Lipschits, *The Fall and Rise of Jerusalem*, 153. The influence of this period of Benjaminite residency may be seen in the prayer of the Levites in Nehemiah 9. H. G. M. Williamson has argued that this prayer derives from the Judahite population that remained in the homeland during the Neo-Babylonian period ("Structure and Historiography in Nehemiah 9," *Studies in Persian Period History and Historiography* [FAT; Tubingen: Mohr Siebeck, 2004] 117–31. The northern linguistic features of this prayer identified by Gary A. Rendsburg ("The Northern Origin of Nehemiah 9," *Bib* 72 [1991] 348–66) may result from the influence of a regional Benjaminite dialect upon the Judahites who later returned to their former home territories in the early Persian period and from whom the redactor of Nehemiah 9 drew the prayer.
69. There is much to suggest a strong anti-Jerusalemite sentiment arising in the Judahite rural sector in the latter years of the 8th century BCE. In a recent study, I have suggested that rural criticisms of Hezekiah may be sensed in traditions currently embedded in the Pentateuch; see Mark Leuchter, "Genesis 38 in Social and Historical Perspective," forthcoming in *JBL*. Jeremy Schipper has also identified an anti-Hezekiah theme

underlying the book of Kings which was subsequently reworked to direct attention against Manassah; see his essay "Hezekiah, Manasseh and Dynastic or Transgenerational Punishment," *Soundings in Kings*, 81–105. Thus sentiment was ripe already by Josiah's reign for the questioning of Davidic legitimacy in the face of Assyrian hegemony, and this must have only been aggravated by Josiah's assault on the rural sector.

70. Hutton, "All the King's Men."
71. Edelman notes that 1 Samuel 12:1–2 refer the reader back to 1 Samuel 8 (*King Saul*, 67).
72. Here again, Würthwein's model of Deuteronomistic redaction seems to be at work, with trends in the book of Kings being projected back into the book of Samuel, forging connections between the two (Wuthwein, "Erwagungen zum sog. deuteronomistischen Geschichteswerk").
73. This reworking of book of Judges in light of the formation of the book of Samuel further affirms the position of Würthwein, op. cit., though this too is connected to simultaneous similar composition and shaping in Kings.

CONCLUSION

1. See Mark Leuchter, "Ezra's Mission and the Levites of Casiphia," *Community Identity in Judaen Historiography* (ed. Gary N. Knoppers and Kenneth A. Ristau; Eisenbrauns: Winona Lake: Eisenbrauns, 2009) 187–9.
2. For similar observations regarding the relationship between Ezra and Nehemiah in relation to antecedent figures in Israelite tradition, see Sara Japhet, "Periodization between History and Ideology II: Chronology and Ideology in Ezra-Nehemiah," *Judah and the Judeans in the Persian Period* (ed. Oded Lipschits and Manfred Oeming; Winona Lake: Eisenbrauns, 2006) 491–505.
3. With most contemporary scholars, I assume here a fairly lengthy development of Ezra–Nehemiah down into the 4th century BCE and possibly beyond, even if many of the sources found therein derive from the 5th century and emerge from the impact of the titular characters on the Yehudite world of the time.
4. See Mark Leuchter, "Rethinking the Jeremiah 'Doublet' in Ezra–Nehemiah and Chronicles," *What Was Authoritative for Chronicles?* (ed. Ehud Ben Zvi and Diana Edelman; Winona Lake: Eisenbrauns, 2011) 199–200.
5. See, for example, Knoppers, *I Chronicles 1–9*, 83–5 (citing earlier studies therein), where the Chronicler allows the northern populations to share in the Jerusalem cult, especially through the overtures of Hezekiah.

6. Knoppers, *I Chronicles 1–9*, 83–5; Yigal Levin, "Who Was the Chronicler's Audience? A Hint From His Genealogies," *JBL* 124 (2003) 229–45.
7. On the temples' rebuilding as a Persian-sponsored enterprise, see James Trotter, "Was the Second Jerusalem Temple a Primarily Persian Project?," *SJOT* 15 (2001) 276–94. See also Joachim Schaper, "The Jerusalem Temple as an Instrument of Achaemenid Fiscal Administration," *VT* 45 (1995) 528–39; Schaper, *Priester und Leviten*, 147–51.
8. See Sara Japhet, *I & II Chronicles* (SCM; London, 1993) 1054–5, for Samuel as a "stand in" for the judges. Yet the Chronicler does not attempt to completely obscure the earlier tradition where the judges are mentioned, as 2 Chronicles 35:1 ("Josiah kept a Passover to YHWH in Jerusalem...") contains the same lexical formula as the closing notice in 2 Kings 23:23 ("this Passover was observed to YHWH in Jerusalem..."), essentially citing his source material and directing the reader to it.
9. This assumes, with the consensus of most scholars today, that the Chronicler was active in the latter half of the 4th century BCE, i.e., close to the rise of Alexander over Persia.
10. Rabbinic tradition is clear that Ben Sira is not counted among those works of literature that "defile the hands," i.e., which are afforded Scriptural-canonical status (Tos. Yad. 2.13; see also Y. Sanh. 28a; Qoh Rabbah 12.11).
11. Jeremy Corley, "Canonical Assimilation in Ben Sira's portrayal of Joshua and Samuel," *Rewriting Biblical History: Essays on Chronicles and Ben Sira in Honour of Pancratius C. Bentjees* (ed. Jeremy Corley and Harm von Grol; New York/Berlin: De Gruyter, 2011) 57–73.
12. Joshua is not, after all, presented as a priest in the biblical tradition, but rather as a facilitator of priestly authority (Josh 18).
13. See Paul McKechnie, "The Career of Joshua Ben Sira," *JTS* 51 (2000) 20–2, for Ben Sira's place as a Ptolemaic courtier (though, as McKechnie notes, even this post was not free of tension). McKechnie argues that the book was written in Ptolemaic Egypt, though his observations are just as relevant if the book was composed in early Seleucid Jerusalem by someone more conversant with the political culture of the previous Hellenistic regime.
14. The association with Samuel fits nicely with Ben Sira's implicit association of Simon with Nehemiah as well (Sir 50:2–4) with regard to fortifying the city walls.
15. Alex P. Jassen, "Literary and Historical Studies in the Samuel Apocryphon (4Q160)," *JJS* (2008) 21–38.
16. Ibid., 38.

17. Louis H. Feldman, "Josephus' Portrait of Samuel," *Abr-Nahrain* 30 (1992) 108–9.
18. Ibid., 141–2.
19. Ibid., 130.
20. On the date and authorship of *LAB*, see Frederick James Murphy, "Retelling the Bible: Idolatry in Pseudo-Philo," *JBL* 107 (1988) 284–7.
21. Howard Jacobson, "Samuel's Vision in Pseudo-Philo's Liber Antiquitatum Biblicarum," *JBL* 112 (1993) 310–11.
22. Frederick James Murphy, *Pseudo-Philo: Rewriting the Bible* (Oxford/New York: Oxford University Press, 1993) 192. Virtually all scholars recognize the awareness of Persia in Isaiah 40–55, though disagreement persists as to whether these chapters derive from a late exilic writer that anticipated the rise of Persia over Babylon or from a writer already living under early Persian hegemony.
23. Murphy, *Rewriting the Bible*, 191. On the theme of conflict against Roman oppression, see Saul M. Olyan, "The Israelites Debate Their Options at the Sea of Reeds: LAB 10:3, Its Parallels, and Pseudo-Philo's Ideology and Background," *JBL* 110 (1991) 83–91.
24. The relevant text reads as follows: "'WHO SLAUGHTERED' [implies] only if done, but not at the very outset. But the following contradicts it: And he shall slaughter: [this teaches that] slaughtering by a foreigner is valid, for slaughtering by foreigners, women, slaves, and unclean persons is valid, even in the case of most sacred sacrifices. Yet perhaps that is not so, but rather [it must be done] by priests? You can answer: Whence do you come [to propose this]? From the fact that it is said, 'And thou and thy sons with thee shall keep the priesthood in everything that pertaineth to the altar' [Num 18:7], you might think that this applies to slaughter too. Therefore Scripture states, 'And he shall kill the bullock before YHWH; and Aaron's sons, the priests, shall present the blood' [Lev 1:5]: from receiving onwards priesthood is prescribed, which teaches that slaughter by any person is valid."
25. See David Daube, *The New Testament and Rabbinic Judaism* (Salem: Ayers, 1992 [original, London: Athlone, 1956]) 14, who considers the possibility of this earlier origin but is hesitant to assign it a date.
26. See further below re: the similar Jesus legend in Luke.
27. On the hermeneutical rules of the Rabbis, see Hermann L. Strack and Günter Stemberger, *Introduction to the Talmud and Midrash* (trans. Markus Bockmuehl; Minneapolis: Fortress Press, 1996) 15–30.
28. *Kiddushin* 49b. See also *Menachot* 29b, where it is the 2nd–century CE sage Akivah who teaches *torah* to no less than Moses.

29. Matthew J. Grey, "The Preservation of Priestly Lineage after 70 CE," paper presented at the 2011 Annual Meeting of the Society of Biblical Literature.
30. Seth Schwartz, *Imperialism and Jewish Society, 200 BCE–640 CE* (Princeton/Oxford: Princeton University Press, 2001) 110–28.
31. On the cosmopolitan nature of the Patriarchate, see Amram Tropper, *Wisdom, Politics and Historiography: Tractate Avot in the Context of the Greco-Roman Near East* (Oxford: Oxford University Press, 2004). On the expansion of the Rabbis into the synagogues in late antiquity, see Schwartz, *Imperialism and Jewish Society*, 259–74.
32. Daube, *Rabbinic Judaism*, 15–16. See also Acts 3:24; 13:20; Heb 11:32.
33. John T. Carroll, "Luke's portrayal of the Pharisees," *CBQ* 50 (1988) 604–21.
34. Daube refrains from determining whether or not Luke draws from the tradition preserved in *Berakhot* 31b (*Rabbinic Judaism*, 16). It remains possible that both derive from a common source and work it in different directions, but the predilection in Luke–Acts to countenance and challenge Pharisaic and rabbinic tradition seems, to my mind, suggestive of the Lukan author's conscious decision to appropriate and redefine the terms of an older tradition regarding Samuel for similar purposes.

Bibliography

Ackerman, Susan "Why Is Miriam Also Among the Prophets? (And Is Zipporah Among the Priests?)," *JBL* 121 (2002) 47–80.

Ahlström, Gösta W. *Royal Administration and National Religion in Ancient Palestine* (Leiden: Brill, 1982).

Amit, Yaira "The Saul Polemic in the Persian Period," *Judah and the Judeans in the Persian Period* (ed. Oded Lipschits and Manfred Oeming; Winona Lake: Eisenbrauns, 2006) 647–61.

Assman, Jan *Moses The Egyptian: The Memory of Egypt in Western Monotheism* (Cambridge, MA: Harvard University Press, 1997).

Baden, Joel S. "The Violent Origins of the Levites Text and Tradition," *Levites and Priests in Biblical History and Tradition* (ed. Jeremy M. Hutton and Mark Leuchter; Atlanta: SBL, 2011) 103–16.

Barmash, Pamela "At the Nexus of History and Memory: The Ten Lost Tribes," *AJS Review* 29 (2005) 207–36.

Barstad, Hans *The Religious Polemics of Amos* (Leiden: Brill, 1984).

―― "The Understanding of the Prophets in Deuteronomy," *SJOT* 8 (1994) 236–51.

Barton, John *Amos's Oracles Against the Nations* (Cambridge: Cambridge University Press, 1980).

Bedford, Peter R. *Temple Restoration in Early Achaemenid Persia* (JSJSup; Leiden: Brill, 2001).

Ben Zvi, Ehud 'The Prophets'—References to Generic Prophets and Their Role in the Construction of the Image of the 'Prophets of Old' within the Postmonarchic Readership/s of the Book of Kings," *ZAW* 116 (2004) 555–67.

―― "Reconstructing the Intellectual Discourse of Ancient Yehud," *Studies in Religion* 39 (2010) 7–23.

Ben-Barak, Z. "The Mizpah Covenant: The Source of the Israelite Monarchic Covenant," *ZAW* 91 (1979) 30–43.

Berman, Joshua *Created Equal: How the Bible Broke with Ancient Political Thought* (New York/Oxford: Oxford University Press, 2008).

Beyerlin W. "Das Konigscharisma bei Saul," *ZAW* 73 (1961) 187–90.

Blenkinsopp, Joseph *A History of Prophecy in Israel* (Louisville: Westminster John Knox, 1996).

Bodner, Keith *1 Samuel: A Narrative Commentary* (Sheffield: Sheffield Phoenix Press, 2008).

Brettler, Marc Zvi *The Creation of History in Ancient Israel* (London: Routledge, 1995).
Byrne, Ryan "The Refuge of Scribalism in Iron I Palestine," *BASOR* 345 (2007) 1–31.
Campbell Antony F. *Of Prophets and Kings: A Late Ninth-Century Document (1 Samuel 1–2 Kings 10)* (CBQMS; Washington D.C.: CBA, 1986)
Carr, David M. *Writing on the Tablet of the Heart: Origins of Scripture and Literature* (New York/Oxford: Oxford University Press, 2005)
Carroll, John T. "Luke's Portrayal of the Pharisees," *CBQ* 50 (1988) 604–21.
Chaney, Marvin L. "Micah—Models Matter: Political Economy and Micah 6:9–15," *Ancient Israel: The Old Testament in its Social Context* (ed. Philip F. Esler; Minneapolis: Augsberg Fortress, 2006) 145–60.
Chavel, Simeon "Oracular Novellae and Biblical Historiography: Through the Lens of Law and Narrative," *Clio* 39 (2009) 1–27.
Cole, Stephen W. (with Peter M. Machinist) (ed.) *Letters from Priests to the Kings Esarhaddon and Assurbanipal* (SAA; Helsinki: Helsinki University Press, 1998).
Cook, Stephen L. *The Social Roots of Biblical Yahwism* (Atlanta: SBL, 2004).
Corley, Jeremy "Canonical Assimilation in Ben Sira's portrayal of Joshua and Samuel," *Rewriting Biblical History: Essays on Chronicles and Ben Sira in Honour of Pancratius C. Bentjees* (ed. Jeremy Corley and Harm von Grol; New York/Berlin: De Gruyter, 2011) 57–73.
Couey, Blake "Amos vii 10–17 and Royal Attitudes Toward Prophecy in the Ancient Near East," *VT* 58 (2008) 300–14.
Cross, Frank Moore *Canaanite Myth and Hebrew Epic* (Cambridge, MA: Harvard University Press, 1973).
Daube, David *The New Testament and Rabbinic Judaism* (Salem: Ayers, 1992 [original, London: Athlone, 1956]).
de Hoop, Raymond "Judges 5 Reconsidered: Which Tribes? What Land? Whose Song?," *The Land of Israel in Bible, History and Theology* (ed. J. Van Ruiten and J. C. De Vos, VTSup; Leiden: Brill, 2009) 151–66.
De Jong, Matthjis *Isaiah Among the Ancient near Eastern Prophets* (VTSup; Leiden: Brill, 2007).
Dearman, J. Andrew "My Servants the Scribes: Composition and Context in Jeremiah 36," *JBL* 109 (1990) 403–21.
Dever, William G. *Who Were The Early Israelites and Where Did They Come From?* (Grand Rapids: Eerdmans, 2003).
Dietrich, Walter *Prophetie und Geschichte: Eine redaktionsgeschichtliche Untersuchung zum deuteronomistichen Geschichtswerk* (FRLANT; Gottingen: Vandenhoek&Ruprecht, 1972).

—— "Prophetie im deuteronomistichen Geschichtswerk," *The Future of the Deuteronomistic History* (ed. Thomas Romer, BETL; Leuven: Leuven University Press 2000) 47–65.

—— *The Early Monarchy in Israel: The Tenth Century B.C.E.* (Atlanta: SBL, 2007; original, 1997).

Dijkstra, Meindert "Moses, the Man of God," *The Interpretation of Exodus: Essays in Honour of Cornelis Houtman* (ed. Riemer Roukema et al.; Leuven: Peeters, 2006) 17–36.

Dus, Jan "Die Geburtslegende Samuels, I Sam 1: Eine traditionsgeschichtliche Untersuchung zu 1 Sam 1–3," *Revista degli Studi Orientali* 43 (1968) 163–94.

Dutcher-Walls Patricia, "The Social Location of the Deuteronomists: A Sociological Study of Factional Politics in Late Pre-Exilic Judah," *JSOT* 52 (1991) 77–94.

Edelman Diana V. *King Saul in the Historiography of Judah* (JSOTSup; Sheffield: Sheffield Academic Press, 1991).

—— "Did Saulide–Davidide Rivalry Resurface in Early Persian Yehud?," *The Land that I Will Show You: Essays on the History and Archaeology of the Ancient Near East in Honor of J. Maxwell Miller* (ed. J. Andrew Dearman and M. Patrick Graham, JSOTSup; Sheffield: Sheffield Academic Press, 2001) 77–83.

—— "Of Priests and Prophets and Interpreting the Past: The Egyptian *Hm-Ntr* and *Hry-Hbt* and the Judahite *Nabi*'," *The Historian and the Bible: Essays in Honour of Lester L. Grabbe* (LHBOTS, ed. Philip R. Davies and Diana V. Edelman; London: T & T Clark 2010) 103–11.

Eslinger, Lyle *Kingship of God in Crisis* (Decatur: JSOT Press, 1985).

Exum, J. Cheryl "The Center Cannot Hold: Thematic and Textual Instabilities in Judges," *CBQ* 52 (1990) 410–31.

Eynikel, Erik "Judges 19–21, An Appendix: Rape, Murder, War and Abduction," *Communio Viatorum* 47 (2005) 100–15.

Feldman, Louis H. "Josephus' Portrait of Samuel," *Abr-Nahrain* 30 (1992) 108–9.

—— *Remember Amalek!: Vengeance, Zealotry and Group Destruction in the Bible according to Philo, Pseudo-Philo and Josephus* (Cincinatti: Hebrew Union College Press, 2004).

Finkelstein, Israel (with Neil Asher Silberman) "Temple and Dynasty: Hezekiah, the Remaking of Judah, and the Rise of the Pan-Israelite Ideology," *JSOT* 30.3 (2006) 259–85.

Fishbane, Michael *Biblical Interpretation in Ancient Israel* (Oxford: Clarendon, 1985).

Flanagan, James W. "Chiefs in Israel," *JSOT* 20 (1981) 47–73.

Fleming, Daniel E. "Mari and the Possibilities of Biblical Memory," *RA* 92 (1998) 41–78.

——*Democracy's Ancient Ancestors: Mari and Early Collective Governance* (New York/Cambridge: Cambridge University Press, 2004).

——"Southern Mesopotamian Titles for Temple Personnel in the Mari Archives," *Inspired Speech: Prophecy in the Ancient Near East* (ed. John Kaltner and Louis Stulman, JSOTSup; London/New York: T and T Clark, 2004) 72–81.

Friedman, Richard Elliott "From Egypt to Egypt: Dtr1 and Dtr2," *Traditions in Transformation*: Turning Points In Biblical Faith (ed. Baruch Halpern and Jon D. Levenson; Winona Lake: Eisenbrauns, 1981) 167–92.

Frolov, Serge "The Semiotics of Covert Action in 1 Samuel 9–10," *JSOT* 31.4 (2007) 429–50.

Galvin, Garett *Egypt as a Place of Refuge* (FAT; Tübingen: Mohr Siebeck, 2011).

Garsiel, Moshe "The Book of Samuel: Its Composition, Structure and Significance as a Historiographical Source," *Journal of Hebrew Scriptures* 10 (2010) Article 5; online at http://www.jhsonline.org

Geoghegan, Jeffrey C. *The Time, Place and Purpose of the Deuteronomistic History: The Evidence of "Until This Day"* (BJS; Providence: Brown University, 2006).

Gese, H. "Zur Geschichte der Kultsanger am zweiten Tempel," *Abraham unser Vater: Juden und Christen im Gespracheuber der Bibel* (Leiden: Brill, 1963) 222–34.

Gilmour, Rachelle *Representing The Past: A Literary Analysis of Narrative Historiography in the Book of Samuel* (VTSup; Leiden/Boston: Brill, 2011).

Glatt-Gilad, David A. "The Personal Names in Jeremiah as a Source for the History of the Period," *Hebrew Studies* 41 (2000) 31–45.

Grabbe, Lester L. "Sanhedrin, Sanhdriyyot, or Mere Invention?," *JSJ* 39 (2008) 1–19.

——"Shaman, Preacher, or Spirit Medium? The Israelite Prophet in the Light of Anthropological Models," *Prophecy and Prophets in Ancient Israel* (ed. John Day, LHBOTS; London: T & T Clark, 2010) 117–32.

Greer, Jonathan S. "A Marzeah and a Mizraq: A Prophet's Mêlée with Religious Diversity in Amos 6.4–7," *JSOT* 32.2 (2007) 243–62.

Gunneweg, A. H. G. *Leviten und Priester: Hauptlinien der Traditionsbildung und Geschichte des israelitisch-judischen Kultpersonals* (FRLANT; Gottingen: Vandenhoeck & Ruprecht, 1965).

Halpern, Baruch "Brisker Pipes Than Poetry: The Development of Israelite Monotheism," *Judaic Perspectives on Ancient Israel* (ed. Jacob Neusner et al.; Philadelphia: Fortress Press, 1987) 77–115.

—— (with David S. Vanderhooft,) "The Editions of Kings in the 7th and 6th Centuries B.C.E.," *HUCA* 62 (1991) 179–244.

—— "Jerusalem and the Lineages in the Seventh Century BCE: Kinship and the Rise of Individual Moral Liability," *Law and Ideology in Monarchic Israel* (ed. Baruch Halpern and Deborah W. Hobson, JSOTSup; Sheffield: Sheffield Academic Press, 1991) 11–107.

—— *David's Secret Demons: Messiah, Murderer, Traitor, King* (Grand Rapids: Eerdmans, 2001).

—— "Late Israelite Astronomies and the Early Greeks," *Symbiosis, Symbolism, and the Power of the Past* (ed. W.G. Dever and S. Gitin; Winona Lake: Eisenbrauns, 2003) 323–52.

Hamori, Esther "The Spirit of Falsehood," *CBQ* 72 (2010) 15–30.

—— "The Prophet and the Necromancer: Women's Divination for Kings," forthcoming in *JBL*.

Hanson, Paul D. "Zechariah 9 and the Recapitulation of an Ancient Ritual Pattern," *JBL* 92 (1973) 52–3.

Haran, Menahem *Temples and Temple Service Ancient Israel* (Oxford: Clarendon, 1978).

Hauer, Christopher "Does 1 Samuel 9:1–11:15 Reflect the Extension of Saul's Dominion?," *JBL* 86 [1967] 306–10.

Heffelfinger, Katie M. "'My Father is King': Chiefly Politics and the Rise and Fall of Abimelech," *JSOT* 33.3 (2009) 277–92.

Heller, Roy L. *Power, Politics and Prophecy: The Character of Samuel and the Deuteronomistic Evaluation of Prophecy* (London/New York: T & T Clark, 2006).

Hendel, Ronald "The Exodus in Biblical Memory," *JBL* 120 (2001) 601–22.

—— "Cultural Memory," *Reading Genesis: Ten Methods* (New York/Cambridge: Cambridge University Press, 2010) 28–46.

Hiebert, Theodore *The Yahwist's Landscape: Nature and Religion in Early Israel* (New York/Oxford: Oxford University Press, 1996).

Hobson, Russell "Jeremiah 41 and the Ammonite Alliance," *Journal of Hebrew Scriptures* 10 (2010) Article 7; online at http://www.jhsonline.org

Hoffman, Yair "A North Israelite Typological Myth and a Judaen Historical Tradition: The Exodus in Hosea and Amos," *VT* 39 (1989) 169–82.

Holladay, William L. "Elusive Deuteronomists, Jeremiah and Proto-Deuteronomy," *CBQ* 66 (2004) 55–77.

Holloway, Steven W. *Aššur is King! Aššur is King! Religion in the Exercise of Power in the Neo-Assyrian Empire* (Leiden: Brill, 2002).

Houston, Walter L. "Was there a Social Crisis in the Eighth Century?" *In Search of Pre-Exilic Israel* (ed. J. Day, JSOTSup; London/New York: T & T Clark, 2004) 130–47.

Hutton, Jeremy M. "The Levitical Diaspora (I): A Sociological Comparison with Morocco's Ahansal," *Exploring the Longue Durée: Essays in Honor of Lawrence E. Stager* (ed. J. D. Schloen; Winona Lake: Eisenbrauns, 2009) 223–34.

—— *The Transjordanian Palimpsest: The Overwritten Texts of Personal Exile and Transformation in the Deuteronomistic History* (BZAW; Berlin: De Gruyter, 2009).

—— "The Levitical Diaspora (II): Modern Perspectives on the Levitical Cities Lists (A Review of Opinions)," *Levites and Priests in Biblical History and Tradition* (ed. Mark Leuchter and Jeremy M. Hutton; Atlanta: SBL, 2011).

—— "All the King's Men: The Families of the Priests in Cross-Cultural Perspective," *"Seitenblicke": Literarische und historische Studien zu Nebenfiguren im zweiten Samuelbuch* (ed. Walter Dietrich. OBO; Fribourg and Göttingen: Academic Press and Vandenhoeck & Ruprecht, 2011) 121–51.

Jacobs, Jonathan "The Role of the Secondary Characters in the Story of the Anointing of Saul (1 Samuel ix–x)," *VT* 58 (2008) 495–509.

Jacobsen, Thorkild "The Graven Image," *Ancient Israelite Religion: Essays in Honor of Frank Moore Cross* (ed. Patrick D. Miller et al.; Minneapolis: Fortress Press, 1987) 15–29.

Jacobson, Howard "Samuel's Vision in Pseudo-Philo's Liber Antiquitatum Biblicarum," *JBL* 112 (1993) 310–11.

Jamieson-Drake, David W. *Scribes and Schools in Monarchic Judah: A Socio-Archaeological Approach* (JSOTSup; Sheffield: Sheffield Academic Press, 1991).

Japhet, Sara *I & II Chronicles* (OTL; London: SCM Press, 1993).

—— "Periodization between History and Ideology II: Chronology and Ideology in Ezra-Nehemiah," *Judah and the Judeans in the Persian Period* (ed. Oded Lipschits and Manfred Oeming; Winona Lake: Eisenbrauns, 2006) 491–505.

Jassen, Alex P. "Literary and Historical Studies in the Samuel Apocryphon (4Q_160)," *JJS* (2008) 21–38.

Jobling, David *1 Samuel* (Berit Olam; Collegeville: Liturgical Press, 1998).

Jonker, Louis C. "Reforming History: The Hermeneutical Significance of the Book of Chronicles," *VT* 57 (2007) 21–44.

Kallai, Zechariah "Biblical Historiography and Literary History; A Programmatic Survey," *VT* 49 (1999) 338–50.

Knohl, Israel *The Sanctuary of Silence: The Priestly Torah and the Holiness School* (Minneapolis: Fortress Press, 1995).

Knoppers, Gary N. *Two Nations Under God: The Deuteronomistic History of Solomon and the Dual Monarchies* (2 vols., HSM; Atlanta: Scholars, 1994).

—— "Rethinking the Relationship Between Deuteronomy and the Deuteronomistic History: The Case of Kings," *CBQ* 63 (2001) 397–412.

—— *I Chronicles 1–9* (AB; New York: Doubleday, 2003).

Kratz, Reinhard G. *The Composition of the Narrative Books of the Old Testament* (London: T & T Clark, 2005).

Kreutzer, Siegfried "Saul—Not Always—At War: A New Perspective on the Rise of Kingship in Israel," *Saul in Story and Tradition* (ed. Carl S. Ehrlich and Marsha C. White, FAT; Tübingen: Mohr Siebeck, 2006) 39–56.

Laato, Antti "The Levitical Genealogies in 1 Chronicles 5–6 and the Formation of Levitical Ideology in Post-Exilic Judah," *JSOT* 62 (1994) 77–99.

Lalleman-de Winkel, H. *Jeremiah in Prophetic Tradition: An Examination of the Book of Jeremiah in the Light of Israel's Prophetic Traditions* (Leuven: Peeters, 2000).

Lehmann, Gunnar "The United Monarchy in the Countryside: Jerusalem, Judah and the Shephelah in the Tenth Century B.C.E.," *Jerusalem in Bible and Archaeology: The First Temple Period* (ed. Andrew G. Vaughn and Ann E. Killebrew; Atlanta: SBL, 2003) 117–63.

Leuchter Mark "A King Like All the Nations: The Composition of I Sam 8, 11–18," *ZAW* 117 (2005) 543–58).

—— "The Literary Strata and Narrative Sources of Psalm xcix," *VT* 55 (2005) 18–36.

—— "Jeroboam the Ephratite," *JBL* 125 (2006) 51–72.

—— *Josiah's Reform and Jeremiah's Scroll: Historical Calamity and Prophetic Response* (Sheffield: Sheffield Phoenix Press, 2006).

—— "Something Old, Something Older: Reconsidering 1 Samuel 2:27–36," *Perspectives on Hebrew Scriptures* (ed. Ehud Ben Zvi; Piscataway: Gorgias Press, 2006) 533–40.

—— "Now There Was a [Certain] Man: Compositional Chronology in Judges–1 Samuel," *CBQ* 69 (2007) 429–39.

—— "Why is the Song of Moses in the Book of Deuteronomy?" *VT* 57 (2007) 295–317.

—— *The Polemics of Exile in Jeremiah 26–45* (New York/Cambridge: Cambridge University Press, 2008).

—— "Ezra's Mission and the Levites of Casiphia," *Community Identity in Judaen Historiography* (ed. Gary N. Knoppers and Kenneth A. Ristau; Winona Lake: Eisenbrauns, 2009) 173–95.

—— "The 'Prophets' and the 'Levites' in Josiah's Covenant Ceremony," *ZAW* 121 (2009) 31–47.

—— (with Klaus-Peter Adam) "Introduction," *Soundings in Kings: Perspectives and Methods in Contemporary Scholarship* (ed. Mark Leuchter and Klaus-Peter Adam; Minneapolis: Fortress Press, 2010) 1–11.

Leuchter Mark "The Sociolinguistic and Rhetorical Implications of the Source Citations in Kings," *Soundings in Kings*, 119–34.
—— "'Why Tarry the Wheels of His Chariot?' (Judg 5,28): Canaanite Chariots and Echoes of Egypt in the Song of Deborah," *Bib* 91 (2010) 256–68.
—— "Eisodus as Exodus: The Song of the Sea (Exod 15) Reconsidered," *Bib* 92 (2011) 321–46.
—— "Rethinking the Jeremiah 'Doublet' in Ezra–Nehemiah and Chronicles," *What Was Authoritative for Chronicles?* (ed. Ehud Ben Zvi and Diana Edelman; Winona Lake: Eisenbrauns, 2011) 183–200.
—— "Genesis 38 in Social and Historical Perspective," forthcoming in *JBL*.
—— "The Fightin' Mushites," *VT* 62 (2012) 479–500.
Levin, Yigal "Who Was the Chronicler's Audience? A Hint From His Genealogies," *JBL* 124 (2003) 229–45.
Levinson, Bernard M. *Deuteronomy and the Hermeneutics of Legal Innovation* (New York/Oxford: Oxford University Press, 1997).
—— "The Reconceptualization of Kingship in Deuteronomy and the Deuteronomistic History's Transformation of Torah," *VT* 51 (2001) 511–34.
—— "The Manumission of Hermeneutics: The Slave Laws of the Pentateuch as a Challenge to Contemporary Pentateuchal Theory," *Congress Volume 2004* (ed. Andre Lemaire, VTSup; Leiden: Brill, 2006) 281–324.
Lewis, Theodore J. "Family, Household and Local Religion in Late Bronze Age Ugarit," *Household and Family Religion in Antiquity* (ed. John Bodel and Saul M. Olyan; Malden, MA/Oxford: Blackwell, 2008) 60–88.
Lipschits, Oded *The Fall and Rise of Jerusalem* (Winona Lake: Eisenbrauns, 2005).
Lohfink, Norbert "Die Sicherung der Wirksamkeit des Gotteswortes durch das Prinzip das Schriftlichkeit der Tora und das Prinzip der Gewaltenteilung nach der Ämtergesetzen des Buches Deuteronomium (Dt 16, 18–18, 22)" *Studien zum Deuteronomium und zur deuteronomistichen Literatur*, vol. 1 (SBAB; Stuttgart: Katholisches Bibelwerk, 1990) 305–23.
—— "Der jungende Jeremia als Propagandist und Poet: zum Grundstock von Jer 30–31," *Le Livre de Jeremie: Le prophete et son milieu* (ed. P. M. Bogaert, BETL; Leuven: Peeters, 1997 [original, 1981]) 351–68.
Long, Burke O. "Social Dimensions of Prophetic Conflict," *Semeia* 21 (1982) 31–43.
Lundbom, J. R. "The *Inclusio* and Other Framing Devices in Deuteronomy i–xviii," *VT* 46 (1996) 296–315.
McAlpine, Thomas H. *Sleep, Divine and Human in the Old Testament* (JSOTSup; Sheffield: JSOT Press, 1987).
McCarter, P. Kyle *I Samuel* (AB; Garden City: Doubleday, 1980).

McKechnie, Paul "The Career of Joshua Ben Sira," *JTS* 51 (2000) 3–26.
Mendelsohn, I. "Samuel's Denunciation of Kingship in Light of the Akkadian Documents from Ugarit," *BASOR* 143 (1956) 17–22.
Meyers, Carol "David as Temple Builder," *Ancient Israelite Religion: Essays in Honor of Frank Moore Cross* (ed. Patrick D. Miller et al.; Minneapolis: Fortress Press, 1987) 357–72.
—— *Discovering Eve: Ancient Israelite Women in Context* (New York: Oxford University Press, 1988) 220–71.
—— "Kinship and Kingship: The Early Monarchy," *The Oxford History of Biblical Israel* (ed. Michael D. Coogan; New York/Oxford: Oxford University Press, 1998).
Miller, Robert D. *Chieftains of the Highland Clans: A History of Israel in the Twelfth and Eleventh Centuries B.C.* (Grand Rapids: Eerdmans, 2005).
—— "When Pharaohs Ruled: On the Interpretation of Judges 5:2," *JTS* 59 (2008) 650–4.
Milstein, Sarah "Reworking Ancient Texts: Revision Through Introduction in Biblical and Mesopotamian Literature" (Ph.D. Diss., New York University, 2010).
Mobley, Gregory *The Empty Men: The Heroic Tradition of Ancient Israel* (New York: Doubleday, 2005).
—— *Samson and the Liminal Hero in the Ancient Near East* (New York/London: T & T Clark, 2006).
Mohlenbrink, Kurt "Die levitischen Uberlieferungen des Alten Testaments," *ZAW* n.s. 11 (1934) 184–231.
Monroe, Lauren A.S. *Josiah's Reform and the Dynamics of Defilement* (New York/Oxford: Oxford University Press, 2010).
Murphy, Frederick James "Retelling the Bible: Idolatry in Pseudo-Philo," *JBL* 107 (1988) 275–87.
—— Pseudo-Philo: Rewriting the Bible (Oxford/New York: Oxford University Press, 1993).
Na'aman, Nadav "When and How Did Jerusalem Become a Great City? The Rise of Jerusalem as Judah's Premier City in the Eighth–Seventh Centuries B.C.E.," *BASOR* 347 (2007) 21–48.
—— "The Israelite-Judahite Struggle for the Patrimony of Ancient Israel," *Bib* 91 (2010) 1–23.
Nelson, Richard D. "The Double Redaction of the Deuteronomistic History: The Case Is Still Compelling" *JSOT* 29.3 (2005) 319–37.
Nihan, Christophe "The Holiness Code Between D and P: Some Comments on the Function and Significance of Leviticus 17–26 in the Composition of the Torah," *Deuteronomium Zwischen Pentateuch und deuteronomischen*

Geschichtewerk (ed. Eckart Otto and Reinhard Achenbach, FRLANT; Göttingen: Vandenhoeck and Ruprecht, 2004) 81–122.

Nihan, Christophe "Saul Among the Prophets (1 Sam 10:10–12 and 19:18–24): The Reworking of Saul's Figure in the Context of the Debate on 'Charismatic Prophecy' in the Persian Era," *Saul in Story and Tradition* (ed. Carl S. Erlich and Marsha C. White, FAT; Tubingen: Mohr Siebeck, 2006) 88–118.

Nissinen, Martti *Prophecy in its Ancient Near Eastern Context: Mesopotamian, Biblical and Arabian Perspectives* (Atlanta: SBL, 2000).

—— "City as Lofty As Heaven: Arbela and Other Cities in Neo-Assyrian Prophecy," *Every City Shall Be Forsaken: Urbanism and Prophecy in Ancient Israel and the Near East* (ed. Lester L. Grabbe and Robert D. Haak; JSOTSup; Sheffield: Sheffield Academic Press, 2001) 172–209.

—— With Robert K. Rittner and C. L. Seow, *Prophets and Prophecy in the Ancient Near East* (Atlanta: SBL, 2003).

Noll, Kurt "Deuteronomistic History or Deuteronomistic Debate? (A Thought Experiment)" *JSOT* 31.3 (2007) 311–45.

Noth, Martin *Uberlieferungsgeschichtliche Studien* (Tübingen: JCM Mohr, 1957 [2nd ed.; original 1943]).

O'Connell, Robert H. *The Rhetoric of the Book of Judges* (VTSup; Leiden: Brill, 1996).

Ollenburger, Benjamin C. *Zion, City of the Great King: A Theological Symbol of the Jerusalem Cult* (JSOTSup; Sheffield: Sheffield Academic Press, 1987).

Olyan, Saul M. "The Israelites Debate their Options at the Sea of Reeds: LAB 10:3, Its Parallels, and Pseudo-Philo's Ideology and Background," *JBL* 110 (1991) 75–91.

Otto, Eckhart "Das Deuteronomium als archimedischer Punkt der Pentateuchkritic: Auf dem weg zueiner Neubergrundung der de Wettes'schen Hypothese," *Deuteronomy and Deuteronomic Literature* (Fs. C. H. W. Brekelmans, ed. M. Vervenne and J. Lust, BETL; Leuven: Leuven University Press, 1997) 321–39.

Pakkala, Juha "The Date of the Oldest Edition of Deuteronomy," *ZAW* 121 (2009) 388–401.

Parker, Simon B. "Possession Trance and Prophecy in Pre-Exilic Israel," *VT* 28 (1978) 271–85.

Peckham, Brian *History and Prophecy: The Development of Late Judean Literary Traditions* (New York: Doubleday, 1993).

—— "Writing and Editing," *Fortunate The Eyes That See: Essays in Honor of David Noel Freedman in Celebration of His Seventieth Birthday* (ed. Astrid B. Beck et al.; Grand Rapids: Eerdmans, 1995) 364–83.

Person, Raymond F. *The Deuteronomistic History and the Book of Chronicles: Scribal Works in an Oral World* (Atlanta: SBL, 2010).
Polzin, Robert *Samuel and the Deuteronomist* (San Francisco: Harper and Row, 1989).
Propp, W. H. C. *Exodus 19–40* (AB; New York: Doubleday, 2006).
Rendsburg Gary A. "The Northern Origin of Nehemiah 9," *Bib* 72 (1991) 348–66.
—— (with William M. Schniedewind) "The Siloam Tunnel Inscription: Historical and Linguistic Perspectives," *IEJ* 60 (2010) 188–203.
Rendtorff, Rolf "Samuel the Prophet: A Link Between Moses and the Kings," *The Quest for Context and Meaning: Studies in Biblical Intertextuality in Honor of James A. Sanders* (ed. Craig A. Evans and Shemaryahu Talmon; Leiden: Brill, 1997) 27–36.
Roberts, Katherine "God, Prophet, and King: Eating and Drinking on the Mountain in First Kings 18:41," *CBQ* 62 (2000) 631–44.
Rofé, Alexander *The Prophetical Stories: The Narratives about the Prophets in the Hebrew Bible, their Literary Types and History* (Jerusalem: Magnes Press, 1988).
—— "Ephraimite versus Deuteronomistic History," *Reconsidering Israel and Judah: Recent Studies on the Deuteronomistic History* (ed. Gary N. Knoppers and J. Gordon McGonville; Winona Lake: Eisenbrauns, 2000) 462–74.
Römer, Thomas C. "Transformations in Deuteronomistic and Biblical Historiographies: On 'Book-Finding' and Other Literary Strategies," *ZAW* 109 (1997) 1–11.
—— *The So-Called Deuteronomistic History* (London: T & T Clark, 2005).
Rütersworden Udo *Von der politischen Gemeinschaft zur Gemeinde: Studien zu Dt 16,18–18,22* (BBB; Frankfurt: Athenaum, 1987).
Sanders, Paul *The Provenance of Deuteronomy 32* (Leiden: Brill, 1996).
Sanders, Seth L. *The Invention of Hebrew* (Urbana: University of Illinois Press, 2009).
Savran, George W. *Encountering the Divine: Theophany in Biblical Narrative* (London: Continuum, 2005).
Schaper, Joachim "The Jerusalem Temple as an Instrument of Achaemenid Fiscal Administration," *VT* 45 (1995) 528–39.
—— *Priester und Leviten im achämenidischen Juda* (FAT; Tübingen: Mohr Siebeck, 2000).
—— "Exilic and Post Exilic Prophecy and the Orality/Literacy Problem," *VT* 55 (2005) 324–42.
Schipper, Jeremy "Hezekiah, Manasseh and Dynastic or Transgenerational Punishment," *Soundings in Kings*, 81–105.

Schley, Donald G. *Shiloh: A Biblical City in Tradition and History* (JSOTSup; Sheffield: Sheffield Academic Press, 1989).

Schloen, J. David "Caravans, Kenites, and Casus Belli: Enmity and Alliance in the Song of Deborah," *CBQ* 55 (1993) 18–38.

—— *The House of the Father as Fact and Symbol: Patrimonialism in Ugarit and the Ancient Near East* (Winona Lake: Eisenbrauns, 2001).

Schniedewind, William M. *Society and the Promise to David* (New York/Oxford: Oxford University Press, 1999).

—— *How The Bible Became A Book: The Textualization of Ancient Israel* (New York/Cambridge: Cambridge University Press, 2004).

Schwartz, Seth *Imperialism and Jewish Society, 200 B.C.E.–640 C.E.* (Princeton: Princeton University Press, 2001).

Seow, C.L. *Myth, Drama, and the Politics of David's Dance* (HSM; Atlanta: Scholars Press, 1989).

Shroter, Ulrich "Jeremias Botschaft fur die Nordreich: zu N. Lohfinks Uberlegungen zum Grundbestand von Jeremia xxx–xxxi," *VT* 35 (1985) 312–29.

Smend, Rudolph "Mose als geschichtliche Gestalt," *HZ* 260 (1995) 1–19.

Smith, Mark S. "El," *Eerdman's Dictionary of the Bible* (ed. David Noel Freedman; Grand Rapids: Eerdmans, 2000) 384–6.

—— *The Origins of Biblical Monotheism* (New York/Oxford: Oxford University Press, 2002).

Sparks, Kenton L. "Israel and the Nomads of Ancient Palestine," *Community Identity in Judean Historiography* (ed. Gerald N. Knoppers and Kenneth A. Ristau; Winona Lake: Eisenbrauns, 2009) 19–26.

Spronk, Klaas "Deborah, a Prophetess: The Meaning and Background of Judges 4:4–5," *The Elusive Prophet: The Prophet as a Historical Person, Literary Character, and Anonymous Artist* (ed. Johannes C. de Moor, VTSup; Leiden: Brill, 2001) 232–42.

Stackert, Jeffrey R. *Rewriting the Torah: Literary Revision in Deuteronomy and the Holiness Legislation* (FAT; Tubingen: Mohr Siebeck, 2007).

Stager, Lawrence E. "The Archaeology of the Family in Ancient Israel," *BASOR* 260 (1985) 1–35.

—— "Forging an Identity: The Emergence of Ancient Israel," in Coogan (ed.) (1998), *The Oxford History of the Biblical World*, 90–129.

Stavrakopoulou, Francesca *King Manasseh and Child Sacrifice: Biblical Distortions of Historical Realities* (BZAW; Berlin: De Gruyter, 2004).

Stern, Philip D. *The Biblical Herem: A Window On Israel's Religious Experience* (BJS; Atlanta: Scholars Press, 1991).

Steussy, Marti J. *Samuel and His God* (Columbia: University of South Carolina Press, 2010).

Strack, Hermann L. (with Günter Stemberger) *Introduction to the Talmud and Midrash* (trans. Marcus Bockmuehl; Minneapolis: Fortress Press, 1996).
Sweeney, Marvin A. *The Twelve Prophets* (Berit Olam; Collegeville: Liturgical Press, 2000).
—— *King Josiah of Judah: The Lost Messiah of Israel* (New York/Oxford: Oxford University Press, 2001).
Taggar-Cohen, Ada "Political Loyalty in the Biblical Account of 1 Samuel xx–xxii in the Light of Hittite Texts," *VT* 55 (2005) 251–68.
Tiemeyer, Lena-Sofia "The Watchman Metaphor in Isaiah lvi–lxvi," *VT* 55 (2005) 378–400.
Tribble, Phyllis *Texts of Terror: A Literary-Feminist Reading of Biblical Narrative* (Minneapolis: Fortress Press, 1984).
Tropper, Amram *Wisdom, Politics and Historiography: Tractate Avot in the Context of the Greco-Roman Near East* (Oxford: Oxford University Press, 2004).
Trotter, James "Was the Second Jerusalem Temple a Primarily Persian Project?," *SJOT* 15 (2001) 276–94.
Tsumura, David T. *The Royal Dynasties in Ancient Israel: A Study on the Formation and Development of Royal-Dynastic Ideology* (BZAW; Berlin: De Gruyter, 1977).
—— *The First Book of Samuel* (NICOT; Grand Rapids: Eerdmans, 2007)
van der Toorn, Karel *Family Religion in Babylonia, Syria and Israel* (Leiden: Brill, 1996).
—— *Scribal Culture and the Making of the Hebrew Bible* (Cambridge, MA: Harvard University Press, 2007).
Weber, Max *The Theory of Social and Economic Organization* (New York: Free Press, 1947).
Weinfeld Moshe *Deuteronomy and the Deuteronomic School* (Oxford: Clarendon, 1972).
—— "Judge and Officer in Ancient Israel," *IOS* 7 (1977) 65–88.
—— *Deuteronomy 1–11* (AB; New York: Doubleday, 1991).
Weippert, Helga "Die deuteronomistischen Beurteilungen der Könige von Israel und Juda und das Problem der Redaktion der Königsbücher," *Bib* 53 (1972) 301–39.
White Marsha C. *The Elijah Legends and Jehu's Coup* (BJS; Atlanta: Scholars Press, 1997).
—— "'The History of Saul's Rise': Saulide State Propaganda in 1 Samuel 1–14," *"A Wise And Discerning Mind": Essays in Honor of Burke O. Long* (ed. Saul M. Olyan and Robert C. Culley, BJS; Providence: Brown University, 2000) 271–92.

Williamson, H. G. M. "The Origins of the Twenty-Four Priestly Courses: A Study of 1 Chronicles xxiii–xxvii," *Studies in the Historical Books of the Old Testament* (ed. J. A. Emerton, VTSup; Leiden: Brill, 1979) 251–68.

—— "Structure and Historiography in Nehemiah 9," *Studies in Persian Period History and Historiography* [FAT; Tubingen: Mohr Siebeck, 2004) 117–31.

—— *Isaiah 1–5* (ICC; London/New York: T & T Clark, 2006).

—— "Prophetesses in the Hebrew Bible," *Prophecy and Prophets in the Hebrew Bible* (ed. John Day; New York/London: T & T Clark, 2010) 65–80.

Willis, Timothy M. "The Nature of Jephtah's Authority," *CBQ* 59 (1997) 33–44.

Wilson Robert R. *Genealogy and History in the Biblical World* (New Haven/London: Yale University Press, 1977).

—— *Prophecy and Society in Ancient Israel* (Minneapolis: Fortress Press, 1980).

Würthwein, Ernst "Erwagungen zum sog. deuteronomistischen Geschichteswerk: Eine Skizze," *Studien Zum Deuteronomistischen Geschichteswerk* (BZAW; Berlin: De Gruyter, 1994) 1–11.

General Index

Abiathar 38–9
Abimelekh 27, 71
agrarian/agrarianism 10, 27–8, 30, 32, 38–9, 45, 58–9, 119, 126
Amalekites 53, 60, 75
Amos 9, 27, 42, 45–6, 55–8, 120–2
Anatoth 39
Assyria/Assyrian 18, 58, 80, 106, 119, 126, 133–4

Babylon/Babylonian 13, 20, 80, 96, 133, 136
Bethel 44, 46, 55–6, 72, 125

Canaan/Canaanite 7, 27–9, 50, 58–60, 76–9, 103, 119
chieftain 68–70, 74–81, 131

Dabar 35, 52, 74, 93, 117–18
Deborah 67, 70–3, 75, 82, 129–30
Deuteronomistic History 10, 13–17, 19–21, 42–3, 46–7, 51–2, 63, 65, 76, 83, 105, 124–5, 129
Deuteronomists 10, 13, 15, 17, 19–21, 32, 38, 49, 61–2, 66–7, 78–82, 104–5, 110, 123–4, 129–30
dream, dream theophany 35–7, 117–18

Egypt, Egyptian/s 7, 58, 77–8, 116, 126, 132, 135
Egypto-Canaanite 27, 60, 77–8
El 6, 35–7
Eli, Elides 8, 31–9, 50–1, 53, 63, 68–9, 92–4, 116, 118, 124
Ezekiel 15, 42, 44–5, 59, 62, 120

genealogy/genealogies 22–5, 74, 84, 112–13, 131
Gideon 27, 68–71, 75, 82, 104, 128–9, 131

Herem 53–4, 60–1, 88, 124, 127

Hosea 9, 28–30, 43–5, 55–8, 69, 74, 115, 121, 125, 128
Huldah 72–3, 129

Jephtah 69–70, 75, 131
Jeremiah 4–5, 29–30, 39, 41–6, 51–2, 62, 102, 108–9, 115, 117, 124–6, 131
Jerusalem 5, 17, 22–4, 29, 42–3, 46–7, 49, 56–7, 72, 80, 84–8, 90, 93–4, 109, 120, 123, 125, 133–5
Jesus 94–6, 136
Josiah 14–19, 23, 49, 72, 85, 87, 106, 108–9, 120, 125, 134
Judge/Judges 8–9, 11, 21, 62–3, 65–75, 78, 81–2, 86, 92, 131–2, 135

kings/kingship 2, 4–5, 9, 14–18, 43, 46–7, 49–51, 54, 60–2, 64–8, 71, 79–81, 84, 87, 89, 91, 100, 106–7, 110, 115, 119, 121, 123, 127

law 7, 9, 11, 15, 18–19, 23–4, 49–50, 62, 64–8, 82, 84, 107, 109, 127
Levite/Levites 5, 8, 10–11, 16–17, 19, 21–35, 37, 39–41, 45, 47, 56, 61–2, 64, 66, 75, 77, 79, 81–2, 86, 107–8, 110–14, 121, 127, 131, 133

Masoretic Text (MT) 12, 37, 51, 116–17, 123–4, 126, 128
Micah 9, 42–3, 56–8
Moses 5, 7–8, 29, 31, 33–4, 36–40, 43, 45–6, 49, 51–2, 65–6, 81, 87–8, 94–5, 102, 114, 116–18, 128, 136
Mushite/s 33, 38, 95, 116

Pentateuch 5, 7–9, 24, 28–9, 37, 65–8, 79, 100, 113, 133
Persia/Persian 11, 23, 80, 83–6, 91, 106, 112, 135–6

priest/s, priesthood, priestly 3–8, 10, 16–17, 19, 21, 23–8, 30–4, 37–41, 43–6, 50–3, 56, 61–3, 65, 68–9, 74, 79, 84, 87–8, 90, 92–5, 100, 102, 104, 107–8, 110, 113, 115–17, 119, 121–2, 125, 127, 135–6
Prophetic Record 14, 100–1, 104, 106, 112, 124, 131
prophets 2–3, 5, 9, 11, 41–7, 49, 52–3, 55–6, 58–62, 64, 70, 74, 78, 94–6, 102, 104–5, 117, 119–22, 125

sacrifice 24, 53–60, 70, 75, 92, 124–6, 136

scribes 9, 15–16, 42–3, 49, 72, 102, 105–8, 121, 125
Septuagint (LXX) 12, 116–17, 123–4, 128
Shiloh 8–10, 31–7, 41, 47–53, 59, 79, 93–4, 118, 122–4
Sinai/Horeb 3, 82, 100

temple 5, 16–17, 19, 22–3, 28, 66, 84–8, 90, 93–5, 104, 109–10, 112, 135

wilderness 7, 28–30, 66, 96, 103, 114–15

Zadok/zadokites 24, 34, 38, 117
Zuph/Zuphite, zopheh 22, 74–5, 102, 130

Scripture Index

Genesis
  1:2 59
  18–19 58
  29:1 7
  29:34 24, 113

Exodus 24, 65
  2:1–10 114
  3 36
  3:6 37
  15 7, 59
  15:4 60
  15:13 38
  15:17 38
  17:1b–7 113–14
  17:8–16 60
  17:14 127
  19:16 3
  19:16–19 73
  28 24
  32:26–9 24, 113
  33:11 37
  39 117

Leviticus 66
  1:5 136
  8 24
  10:11 117
  10:19–20 117
  16 115
  17–26 109
  24 65
  24:10–23 65

Numbers 24, 65
  5 108
  12 36
  12:6–8 33, 37–8, 118
  12:7 33
  18:2 113
  18:7 136

Deuteronomy 29, 49, 66–7, 81, 105–11,
    120, 127–8
  5:4–5 51, 73

  6:5–9 19
  11 127
  11:20 19
  12 16–17
  13 120
  13:2–3 42–3
  16:18–20 18, 66–7
  16:18–18:22 18
  17:8–13 66
  17:9 127–8
  17:11 127–8
  17:13 66
  17:14–20 15–16,
    49, 51, 81
  17:15–16 67
  17:18–20 49, 61
  18:9–14 124
  18:15 119
  18:15–18 84
  18:16 51
  18:18 51–2
  18:19–22 61
  18:20–2 119
  25:17–19 60
  27 127
  30:11–14 19
  31:9–13 127
  31:14 51
  31:23 51
  32:9–10 29
  32:13–14 29
  33:8–11 24, 26, 64
  33:9 27
  33:10 114
  33:11 31
  34:10 37

Joshua 13–14, 16, 20–1, 25, 30, 47
  1:1 51
  1:2–8 48
  7:14–18 130
  8:2 127
  8:30–5 111
  18 47
  18:1 48

Joshua (*cont.*)
  18:10 48
  21:12 50

Judges 9, 11, 20, 47, 49–51, 63, 67–71, 73–6, 78–9, 100, 124, 130–1, 134
  2:11–18 78
  2:11–19 63, 71
  2:18 68
  4 72
  4:4 73
  4:4–5 67, 72, 82
  4–5 70
  5 71, 73, 129
  5:2 78
  5:2–5 7
  5:15 73
  6 70, 130
  6:8–10 70, 82
  6:12 131
  8 71
  8:23–32 68
  8:27 69
  8–9 27
  9 71
  11:1 70, 131
  17–18 111
  17:1–6 111
  17:7–18:31 26
  21 50
  21:12 59
  21:19–24 49
  21:25 111

1 Samuel 4, 23, 34
  1 32
  1:1 22, 39, 74, 111, 131
  1:3 32, 53
  1:9 32
  1:12–14 32
  1:13–14 32
  1:20 6
  2 32
  1–2 32, 34, 102–3
  1–3 23, 31–2, 37–8, 40–1, 44–5, 50, 66, 92, 95
  1–31 1
  2:1–10 91, 115
  2:11 32, 69
  2:12–16 53
  2:12–17 32
  2:13–17 32
  2:18–20 32
  2:22–25 32
  2:27–36 32, 34, 38, 43, 50
  2:27 36
  2:27–8 116
  2:27–9 33
  2:29 33
  2:35 33, 38, 117
  2:36 34
  3 34–5, 37–8, 52, 69, 89, 118
  3:1 50
  3:3–18 50
  3:4–5 36
  3:6 116
  3:10 36
  3:16 116
  3:16–18 118
  3:20 51
  3:21 51–2, 69
  3:22 51
  4 37, 75
  4:1 69
  4:13 32
  4:18 32, 63
  7 67–8, 70, 75, 81, 132
  7:2–13 69
  7:3–4 63, 68
  7:3–14 51
  7:5–13 67
  7:5–12 84
  7:15 69
  7:15–17 66
  7:16–17 68
  7:17 102
  8 67, 71, 84, 119, 128, 134
  8:5 67
  8:11 64
  8:11–18 79
  8:18 61
  8–12 78, 81, 132
  9 78
  9–11 81
  9:1 76–7
  9:1–10:16 2, 31, 76, 100, 115, 131
  9:4–10:9 102
  9:4–5 74
  9:5 74
  9:12–24 53

9:16 131
9:20 89
9:22–4 2
10:10–12 3, 74, 78
10:13 79
10:17–27 51, 130
10:25 23, 51, 64, 66, 84
11 76, 130–1
11:6 74
12 43, 59, 66, 68, 78, 84, 128
12:1–2 51, 134
12:11 69, 81
12:19–23 84
12:21 59–60
13–14 77
13:1 81
13:9 3
13:9–10 53
14:6–15 115
14:14–20 130
14:35 3, 27
15 53–4, 58, 60–1
15:1–2 53
15:9 3
15:10 52
15:22–3 53–4, 61
15:32 127
15:33 60
16:1–13 3, 100
16:1–3 131
16:1–5 55
16:3–5 3
16:18 131
19:20 74
20 133
22 3, 79, 100
9:1–10:16 3
19:18–24 11
19:20 74
28 11, 104

2 Samuel 32, 99
    1–24 1
    3 85
    7:4 52
    8:18 27
    24:11 52

1–2 Kings 15, 42, 61, 81, 85, 134
1 Kings

2:26 24, 39
2:26–7 34, 38
2:35 24
4:4 24
11:28 131
11:29–39 43
12:31 27
13 5
13:1–10 43
13:20 52
19 43
22 42, 46

2 Kings
    9 74
    17:7–23 15
    17:13 54, 61
    17:23 54, 61
    18:1–4 49
    20:4 52
    21:10 61
    22 19, 72
    22:3 18
    22:8–11 17
    22:14 19, 72
    22:14–20 49
    23 16–17
    23:1–3 17
    23:21–3 86
    23:23 135
    23:24 124
    23:33 127
    24:2 61
    24:19 110
    25:7 127

Isaiah 42, 120
    1:10–17 57
    29 43
    40–55 136
    41:29 59
    51:4 91
    66:2 3

Jeremiah 4–5, 30, 42, 44, 46, 109, 115, 125
    1:1 39
    1:9 52
    1:13–19 117
    1:24 117

Scripture Index

Jeremiah (cont.)
  2:2 29
  2:2–3 29
  2–4 109
  3:1–5 43
  7:1–2 117
  7:25 54
  7:31–2 57
  10:1–16 125
  11:1 117
  15:1 4–5, 31, 39, 46, 52
  18:18 44, 46
  19 125
  19:4–6 57
  19:11–14 57
  23:23 37
  25:4 54
  25:21 117
  26–45 15
  26–9 46
  26:5 54
  26:17–19 42
  26:20–3 43
  28 42
  29:5–7 84
  30–1 109
  34:8–22 125
  35:15 54
  36 110
  44 126
  45 124

Ezekiel 42, 120
  7:26 44
  16:3 59
  44:15 24

Hosea 28, 30
  1:1–2 117
  2:16–17 28
  2:23–4 28
  3:1–5 43
  4:1–19 117
  4:6 44
  6:4–7 56
  6:6–7 58
  9:7 44
  9:7–8 74
  9:8 45, 69, 74
  12:11 45
  12:14 45

Amos 46
  3–5 117
  5:21–6 55
  7:10–17 46, 120
  7:10–11 121
  7:13 27, 45, 66
  7:14 46

Micah
  1 117
  3:12 42–3
  6:6–8 56

Habakkuk
  3:5 73

Psalms 5
  29 73
  68 7
  78:60–8 47
  99 5, 102
  99:6 4, 31, 47
  132:6 122

Daniel 88

Ezra–Nehemiah 11, 83–5, 134

Ezra
  7:1–5 84, 131
  7:6 84
  8:15–20 84
  9 84
  9:4 3
  9:11–12 84

Nehemiah
  9 133

1–2 Chronicles 4–5, 8, 11, 23–5, 84–5, 96, 101

1 Chronicles
  11:3 85

2 Chronicles
  34–5 86

35:1 86, 135
35:18 23, 86

Matthew
  4 96
  5 96

Luke–Acts 137
Luke 94, 136–7
  1–2 95
  2:41–7 94
  2:41–52 95
  2:52 94
  4 96

Galatians
  3:28 96

Colossians
  3:11 96

Ben Sira 86
  44–50 86
  45:6–22 87
  46:13–20 87

4Q 160 89

Josephus
  Ant 6.52 89

Pseudo–Philo
  LAB 91
  LAB 51.3–4 91

Mishnah 93
B. Talmud
  Berakhot 10b 94
  Berakhot 31b
    92–5
  Shabbat 113b 92
  Ta'anit 5b 94
  Zebakhim 32a 93

P. Talmud
  Hagigah 77a 94

Midrashim
  ExodR xvi 4 94
  LevR xxii 6 92
  NumR xviii 17 92

The manufacturer's authorised representative in the EU for product safety is
Oxford University Press España S.A. of el Parque Empresarial San Fernando de
Henares, Avenida de Castilla, 2 – 28830 Madrid (www.oup.es/en or product.
safety@oup.com). OUP España S.A. also acts as importer into Spain of products
made by the manufacturer.

www.ingramcontent.com/pod-product-compliance
Ingram Content Group UK Ltd.
Pitfield, Milton Keynes, MK11 3LW, UK
UKHW021259180426
11947UKWH00015B/915